FAIRY HOUSE
CRAFTS

FAIRY HOUSE
CRAFTS

Wonderful, Whimsical Projects for You & Your Fairy House

LIZA GARDNER WALSH

Down East Books
CAMDEN, MAINE

Down East Books

Published by Down East Books
An imprint of The Rowman & Littlefield Publishing Group, Inc.
4501 Forbes Blvd., Ste. 200
Lanham, MD 20706
www.rowman.com

Distributed by NATIONAL BOOK NETWORK

Text copyright © 2018 by Liza Gardner Walsh
Photographs © 2018 Andy Dumas, except Liza Gardner Walsh, 3, 4, 5, 6, 7, 16, 23, 24, 26, 29, 34, 33, 34, 38, 39, 40, 51, 52, 53, 55, 56, 57, 69, 71, 73, 74, 80, 83, 85, 87, 88, 95, 101, 104, 105, 106, 113, 115, 125, 132, 137,139, 140; Bill Petrini, 131; Robinsunne, 65, 67; Dreamstime, 7, 10, 96, 128, 130, 138; iStock, 62, 95, 116; Nithyasrm, 21; JohnnyMrNinja, 25; Neelix, 46; Diane Hill, 47; Wikivisual, 77, 79; Andre Butko, 126; lumpytrout, 127; Whippetsgalore, 136.

Designed by Lynda Chilton, Chilton Creative

British Library Cataloguing-in-Publication Information available

Library of Congress Cataloging-in-Publication Data

Names: Walsh, Liza Gardner, author.
Title: Fairy house crafts and activities / Liza Gardner Walsh.
Description: Camden, Maine : DownEast Book, [2018] | Includes bibliographical references.
Identifiers: LCCN 2017059543 (print) | LCCN 2017060076 (ebook) | ISBN 9781608939626 (e-book) | ISBN 9781608939619 (paperback : alk. paper)
Subjects: LCSH: Dollhouses. | Nature craft. | Fairies in art. | Fairies--Miscellanea.
Classification: LCC T175.3 (ebook) | LCC T175.3 .W348 2018 (print) | DDC 745.592/3--dc23
LC record available at https://lccn.loc.gov/2017059543

ISBN 978-1-60893-961-9 (trade paperback)
ISBN 978-1-60893-962-6 (e-book)

♾™ The paper used in this publication meets the minimum requirements of American National Standard for Information Sciences—Permanence of Paper for Printed Library Materials, ANSI/NISOZ39.48-1992.

Printed in the United States of America.

To my mom, Barbara Gardner, for
sharing her love of tiny things, salt dough,
& cozy days spent making crafts.

Table of Contents

Introduction 11
  Letter to Parents, 13
  Things to Collect, 14
  Tips for Collecting in Nature, 14

1 Natural Craft Supplies 19
  Nature's Glue, 20
  Rice Paste, 21
  Homemade Paints
    • Homemade Watercolor Paint, 22
    • Simple Milk Paint, 22
    • Homemade Poster Paint, 23
    • Faux Oil Paint, 24
    • Egg Tempera Paint, 25
    • Natural Dyes, 27
    • Homemade Seed Paper, 28

2 Fairy House Crafts 31
  Twig Furniture
    • Twig Chair, 33
    • Twig Table, 34
    • Fairy Bed, 35
    • Twig Ladders, 36
    • Fairy Hammock, 37
    • Fairy Broom, 38
  Fireplace, 39
  Sea Shell Sink, 40
  Rugs, 40
  Fairy House Mailbox, 41
  Leaf Envelopes, 42
  Umbrellas
    • Personal Fairy Umbrella, 43
    • Garden Party Umbrella, 45
  Rose Hip Tea Set, 46
  Acorn Tea Set, 47

3   Natural Fairy Dolls ———————————— 51

     Flower Fairy, 52

     Woodland Fairy, 53

     Milkweed Pod Baby Fairy, 55

     Peg People Fairy, 57

     Straw Fairy, 58

     Pine Cone Fairy, 59

4   The Recycled Fairy House ———————— 61

     Robinsunne's Faux Adobe Fairy House, 64

     Robinsunne's Tranlucent Home for a Light Fairy, 66

     Milk Carton Fairy House, 68

     Tiny Books for the Fairies, 69

     Recycled Paper Origami Fairy Chair, 70

     Fused Plastic Bag Rug, 72

5   Fairy Costumes ———————————————— 75

     Wings

       • Traditional Wire Wings, 76

       • Super Easy Fabric Fairy Wings, 78

       • Cardboard Wings, 79

     Fairy Tutus, 81

     Fairy Wands

       • Nature Wand, 83

       • Painted Stripe Wand, 84

       • Flower Fairy Wand, 85

       • Star Wand, 86

     Fairy Slippers, 88

     Flower Crown, 90

     See-through Magic Crown, 91

     Toadstool Purse, 92

     Fairy Dust Pouch Necklace, 93

     Good for the Earth Fairy Dust, 94

     Swirly Sparkly Fairy Dust, 94

6 Your Fairy Room ························· 97

Fairy Doors
- Natural Fairy Door, 98
- Popsicle Stick Fairy Door, 100
- Extra Crafty Fairy Door, 101
- Realistic Clay Fairy Door, 102

Fairy Sleepover Bag, 104
Leaf-Shaped Sleepover Bag, 105
Indoor Fairy Mailbox, 106
Tiny Envelopes, 107
Crafts to Fair-ify Your Room
- Fairy Canopy, 108
- Fairy Flower Curtain, 110
- Painted Flags, 111
- Flower Paper Garland, 112
- Tissue Paper Banner, 113
- Fabric Bunting, 114
- Fairy Lantern, 115
- Fairy Teepee, 117

7 Fairy Gifts Inspired by Nature ··········· 119

Nature Print Wrapping Paper, 120
Flower and Leaf Press, 121
Flower Perfume, 122
Bath Bags, 123
Lavender and Rose Petal Sachets, 124
Sea Shell Candles, 126
Sea Glass Necklace, 127
Birch Bark Pins, 128
Sea Shell Wind Chime, 129

8 Crafts for the Birds & Butterflies

8 Crafts for the Birds & Butterflies 131

    Bird Sipping Station, 133

    Butterfly Feeder, 134

    Cement Bird Bath, 136

    Fairy House Bird House, 137

    Winter Pudding, 138

    Tea Cup Holder, 139

    Suet Cage Nesting Box, 140

    The Winter Tree, 141

Resources 142

Acknowledgments 143

INTRODUCTION

Creativity is contagious. Pass it on.

—Albert Einstein

The paint pots are filled with fresh paint. The glue is at the ready. Paper is neatly stacked in a pile. Buttons, stray ribbons, and tiny shells are lying in wait. Now's the time to roll up your sleeves, pull up a chair, or a place on the lawn, and get ready to create. I imagine you've experienced the magic of making things before. I also assume that since you picked up this particular book, some of this making has included fairy house work. If so, guess what, you are extra creative. Making fairy worlds draws upon all the important skills for a life of crafting—the ability to think outside the box and ask questions. Questions and curiosity are at the heart of creativity, for without asking that first question, "what should I make," nothing happens.

Crafting is a way to make a mark on the world that is truly your own. Each project allows you to use your creativity in a different way. This is not to say it's always easy. Some crafts are tricky. Sometimes the glue isn't quite strong enough or the paper rips or you make a cut you didn't mean to. Sometimes you're not as patient as you were the day before. Sometimes you run out of time before you have to go to soccer practice. And sometimes you spill the paint. But I still believe that, despite any of these issues, there are few better feelings than making something completely from scratch and saying, "I did it." And in this world, where just about everything can be bought, making things is even more important.

But back to fairies. Fairies ooze creativity. They make all kinds of things, including clothing, music, and fairy dust. They also work very hard to create a peaceful, kind, and helpful environment. They truly epitomize the definition of creativity. In this book, I draw upon the fairies' creativity as well as your own inner creative powers. It's a book you can turn to when you've made your fairy house and want to add some special touches. A book that helps you create a fairy oasis in your room and then make a costume for your fairy tea parties. It also guides you in making gifts with flair because fairies love to give. And of course, there's a section that helps the birds and animals because what good would a fairy book be if it didn't help take care of the world.

Just like the fairies, I'm a big fan of nature and protecting our environment. So many of these activities focus on things that are inspired by nature rather than things you can buy in a store. I like to use glitter as much as anyone, but this book is more about nature's glitter, like the sparkle of sea shells or mica or even the soft pink of a rose petal. You will find that many of these crafts use recycled or found materials. There are even natural recipes for common things like glue and paint.

But the biggest wish I have for you as you use this book is that you experience ultimate crafting freedom. Find the projects that speak to you and then create them in whatever way makes you the most excited. You can change things and add new elements—this is just a guide. I give you permission to make a mess and make mistakes because that's where amazing art comes from. But most of all, I want you to have fun. I want you to feel fairy-ish and use the fairies' special magic to help make your creativity soar.

It's not always easy gearing up for a big day of messy crafting. Our lives are busy and already filled to the brim with mess. And maybe you've had the feeling that you missed the creative bus or the artsy genes skipped a generation. All normal feelings. But here's a little nudge, because even if your child is actively creative at school or story time, taking time for crafts is always worth it, even if the results are unexpected or if tears are involved.

I've always felt that making things with my kids was one small way I could slow down and actually be with them amidst the rush of life. Once I committed to setting out the materials and giving a few basic ideas, my kids always managed to take the idea and run with it, leaving my original idea as a mere kernel. I have now worked with thousands of children over the years and it never ceases to amaze me how they come up with better ideas than what we started with. It's humbling in the best way.

But here are a few loose tips. Let your kids lead the way. Back up. Help, but don't hover. Let things fall apart and not work. Let it get messy. Ask questions rather than provide solutions. Focus on the fun, and if it isn't fun, stop and come back to it later or not at all.

While working as a preschool teacher at a Reggio Emilia school, I learned how to talk with kids about their creative process. The first rule is that when looking at a child's piece of art, don't ask, "What is this?" Instead offer one of the following, "Will you tell me more about this?" "Tell me about this line or color." "What do you like best about this particular drawing or project?" "What was the hardest part to draw, assemble or figure out?" "How did you figure it out?" Rather than asking a child to narrowly define their art, these questions allow them to think about the process and open it up.

The second equally important rule is not to say "good job" every minute. There are ample studies by world renowned early childhood educators that cite how pat praise can do more harm than good. Caveat, I have said "good job" a million times to my kids and they are not artistically stunted. Letting kids come up with their own decisions about whether something is good rather than hearing it from us is vital to the creative spirit. If you are in a praise pattern, you can easily change it by simply saying what you saw your child doing. For example, "You made that, you did it, you worked really hard on that." These statements let your child know you were there and that you noticed, and then allows them to freely keep creating without seeking praise.

And lastly, you might not remember the exact moment you made papier mache together, but your kids will always remember that you gave them the time and were willing to take a risk with them. I sure do.

THINGS TO COLLECT

Crafting and collecting are close cousins. There is a good chance that if you like to make things, you're probably one of those kids who can't leave a beach, trail, or yard sale with empty pockets. The beauty of fairy house crafts is that many of them use the interesting bits of nature found all around us. When you look at the world with an eye for crafting and creating, everything is a potential treasure. And each treasure has its own way of fitting into your craft plan. For example, what can you do with an acorn cap or a milkweed pod or those dried seed husks? To be successful in fairy house crafting, it's wise to start stashing some things for a rainy day. Think of it like the pantry in your kitchen. Just as it's helpful to have a little flour, sugar, baking powder, and vanilla around in case you want to bake something, having feathers, shells, and small pieces of bark on hand is great for making fairy house crafts on a whim.

Try to keep your supplies organized if possible. Collection boxes and trays aid in this process, and since you won't be searching for things all day, it will make crafting easier. The following is a list of some natural materials to keep an eye out for, as well as some recyclable materials and other useful trinkets that might appear in the activities in this book. (Note: each activity has a list of materials needed but this is a more general all-purpose craft one.)

TIPS FOR COLLECTING IN NATURE

- Do not pull moss up from the ground. Moss takes many years to grow. For example, pincushion moss can take up to forty years to regenerate if it is disturbed.

- Do not pick flowers from a garden that is not yours unless you have permission. Fairies absolutely adore flowers.

- If you are in a national or state park or at a state beach it is against the law to remove any natural thing.

- Be careful of poison ivy. In the summer it is much harder to see than when it turns red in the fall.

- And one more thing, if you are in nature, certain insects might find you inviting. Always check yourself for ticks after your time in the woods. No one likes ticks, not even fairies.

Natural Materials

The list is long but still does not capture all of the possibilities of materials that are available. Make your own list, add to it constantly.

MICA

MOSS: Only if it is already
    separated from the ground

PINE CONES

BARK: Birch bark is especially useful

STICKS: You can never have
    too many

FEATHERS

SEA GLASS

SHELLS

ROCKS

ACORN CAPS

ROSE HIPS

EGG SHELLS

ABANDONED BIRD'S NESTS:
    They must be abandoned!!!

BERRIES: Never eat a wild berry
    unless you are with a grownup
    who can tell whether it's safe.

GRASS

POPPY PODS

MILKWEED HUSKS

CORN SILK

REEDS

PETALS AND FLOWERS

BEANS AND SEEDS

PUSSY WILLOWS

LAMB'S EAR

HOSTA LEAVES

Trinkets, Found Objects, & Recyclable Materials

- CORKS
- BUTTONS
- POPSICLE STICKS
- BOTTLE CAPS
- MARBLES
- WOOL ROVING & YARN, ROPE & TWINE
- MATCHBOXES
- JEWELRY BOXES
- COTTON BALLS & STUFFING
- PIPE CLEANERS & THIN WIRE

- CARDBOARD
- FABRIC
- FELT
- RIBBON
- BEADS
- MISCELLANEOUS BROKEN JEWELRY
- CRAFT PAPER
- POMPOMS
- FABRIC FLOWERS & LEAVES (we'll use tons of these so stock up when ever you can!)

NATURAL CRAFT SUPPLIES

The fairies certainly don't go to a giant craft store to load up on glue and paint, so why should you? Making your own craft supplies is not only fun and scientific (think kitchen chemistry) but it helps protect our planet. Homemade glue is biodegradable, which means it breaks down into the earth and won't leave a big mess in nature. It is non-toxic, which means it won't make you sick and won't harm plants or animals. And natural glues and paints work well with that all important rule about using only things that come from nature. For example, with rice-based glue, you can glue all the rungs on your fairy ladder and not worry that you are altering nature's delicate balance. Same goes for the home-made paint recipes in this chapter—painting your fairy signs and doors with this stuff will make the fairies jump for joy at your creative and earth-friendly use of color. One last perk, if you run out of paint you will no longer need to ask your parents to take you to the store, you can just head into the kitchen and mix away.

{ Nature's Glue }

YOU WILL NEED

¾ cup water

2 tablespoons corn syrup

1 teaspoon white vinegar

½ cup corn starch

¾ cup ice-cold water

INSTRUCTIONS

STEP 1:   In a small saucepan, mix the water, corn syrup, and vinegar until smooth.

STEP 2:   Heat the mixture over medium heat until it begins to boil.

STEP 3:   Mix corn starch and cold water together in a small bowl and then slowly add this mixture to the saucepan. Stir well.

STEP 4:   Take the saucepan carefully off of the heat and allow to cool. (Make sure a grownup is nearby) Pour into an airtight container and let the glue set overnight before using.

NOTE: To make your glue extra fairy-ish, you can add a little food coloring to jazz it up.

{ Rice Paste }

(Adapted from Green Guide for Artists)

Rice can be very sticky. In fact, there is a type of rice called sticky rice, so no wonder it is used in this glue recipe. A couple of notes about this glue, it's extra thick and doesn't dry clear so it's better for pasting underneath objects where it won't be seen. Known for sticking objects to paper, it makes a great choice for collage work.

NOTE: Rice flour is available in most supermarkets in the gluten-free section.

YOU WILL NEED

¾ cup rice flour

2 tablespoons sugar

¾ cup warm water

INSTRUCTIONS

STEP 1: In a medium saucepan, combine the sugar, rice flour, and water. Stir well until all lumps disappear.

STEP 2: Over low heat, continue stirring until mixture thickens.

STEP 3: Let glue mixture cool and then pour into a jar that has a lid. The glue can be stored for a couple of months.

Homemade Watercolor Paint

YOU WILL NEED

- 3 tablespoons baking soda
- 3 tablespoons cornstarch
- 3 tablespoons white vinegar
- 1½ teaspoons light corn syrup
- Food coloring
- Small plastic or glass containers
  - (like yogurt containers or baby food jars or an ice cube tray)

INSTRUCTIONS

STEP 1: In a small bowl, mix together baking soda, corn starch, and corn syrup.

STEP 2: Pour the mixture into the containers you have handy.

STEP 3: Add one color of food coloring to each jar. Use the watercolors right away in their wet form or let them dry into hard cakes of paint.

Simple Milk Paint

Real milk paint dates back to ancient Egypt and was especially common in Colonial America for painting furniture and barns. But traditional milk paint takes a couple of days to make and requires curdling the milk—Yuck! The following recipe uses condensed milk instead to copy the spirit of milk paint but in a much simpler version.

YOU WILL NEED

- ½ cup condensed milk
- 6 to 8 drops of food coloring.

INSTRUCTIONS

Mix together milk and color or colors of your choice in a small bowl until well-blended. The paint will be high gloss and can be made over and over!

{ Homemade Poster Paint }

ome painters spend a whole day preparing their paints, but in the fairy-craft world, the process is a little easier. You are limited only by how many saucepans you have since each color needs to be created separately.

YOU WILL NEED

- ¼ cup flour
- 1 cup water
- 3 tablespoons of powdered tempera paint for each color
  (this can be tricky to find in regular store. You might need to order it online)
- 2 tablespoons water
- ½ teaspoon liquid starch

INSTRUCTIONS

STEP 1:   In a small saucepan, mix flour and water and stir well.

STEP 2:   Place saucepan over low heat and cook until the mixture begins to thicken. Take off the heat and allow to cool.

STEP 3:   With help from a grownup, pour flour and water mixture into a small bowl then add the powdered tempera and liquid starch. Stir well.

STEP 4:   Keep your paint in an airtight container and paint away.

{ Faux Oil Paint }

This paint is a close second to real oil paint in look and feel but without the strong smell of real oil paint. (Faux is French for fake, by the way.) Another plus about this fake oil paint is that it can be made in less than a minute!

YOU WILL NEED

2 tablespoons clear dishwashing liquid

2 tablespoons powdered tempera paint for each color
(this can be tricky to find in regular store. You might need to order it online)

½ teaspoon water

INSTRUCTIONS

Combine all the ingredients into a small re-sealable container and mix until well-blended.

{ Egg Tempera Paint }

amous artists have painted with egg yolk-based paint for centuries, it's even thought to date back to prehistoric times. Egg tempera is an extremely durable and water-resistant paint and dries quickly. A couple of notes when creating and using this paint: First, use a fresh egg and try not to get any egg white in the mix. Second, this paint won't keep, so only make what you will use.

YOU WILL NEED

Egg yolk (one egg per color)

Pigment (this can be ordered online or bought in art stores. You can also use ground up colored sidewalk chalk)

INSTRUCTIONS

STEP 1: Separate the yolk from the egg. This can be tricky but is a great skill for cooking. Gently rock the yolk from one half of the egg shell to the other to let all of the excess egg white pull away from the yolk.

STEP 2: Place the yolk in a small bowl and use a fork to pierce the yolk.

STEP 3: Mix 1 tablespoon of the pigment and mix well. If the paint feels too thick, add a drop of water.

{ Natural Dyes }

(Adapted from The Green Guide for Artists*)*

You've probably noticed if you've ever picked blackberries how your fingers turn purple. Or if you're a fan of beets, how they turn your fingers red. Although there are only a few crafts in this book that use fabric, knowing how to use natural dyes is a skill you can apply to all kinds of things, including dyeing Easter eggs and even yarn. It's also a great tool for your crafting toolbox.

YOU WILL NEED

A big stockpot that can get stained
(try finding one at a thrift store or yard sale if you plan on doing lots of dyeing)
8 cups of water
1 cup of dye matter (see below)
A wooden spoon

INSTRUCTIONS

The general rule when using natural dyes is to combine 1 cup dye matter to 8 cups of water. Pour the water and the material you are using for the dye into a big stew pot and boil for one hour. Once the dye has cooled, dip your piece of fabric, yarn, or egg, into the pot to test how strong the color is. The color will continue to get stronger the longer it sits so if you want a deeper color just wait a little longer. Below is a list of various plants, fruits, and vegetables you can use to create your dye.

FOR RED
Strawberries, cherries, beets, rosehips
FOR GREEN
Grass, spinach, crabapple leaves
FOR YELLOW
Turmeric powder, dandelion flowers
FOR BLUE AND PURPLE
Blueberries, blackberries, red onion skins, and elderberries
FOR BROWN
Coffee grounds, paprika, yellow onion skin

{ Homemade Seed Paper }

(Adapted from NASA's website for kids: climatekids.nasa.gov)

Making fairy wishes or writing notes to the fairies on paper filled with flower seeds is not only a good thing for the earth but a good way to make sure your wish or note will make it to a fairy.

NOTE: This recipe starts the night before you actually make the paper.

YOU WILL NEED

3 to 4 cups of shredded recycled paper
(If you don't have access to a shredder, you can cut it in thin strips, it just takes a little while)

Large bowl of warm water

Window screen material

Small embroidery hoop

Blender

9- x 13-inch baking pan

Packet of wildflower seeds

Bath towels

Waxed paper

INSTRUCTIONS

STEP 1: Soak the shredded paper over night in a medium-size bowl of warm water.

STEP 2: The next day when you are ready to make your seed paper, fill a blender halfway with the soggy paper and then fill the rest of the blender with water. Blend until the mixture looks like soup.

STEP 3: Pour water into the 9 x 13 pan, until it is about a quarter full, then pour in the blended soupy paper mixture—also called pulp.

STEP 4: Put the window screen in between the embroidery hoop. Dip the screened hoop in from the side so that it slides beneath the pulp. Lift the screen slowly so that you catch the pulp evenly on top and the water drains through the screen. Lay the screen on the bath towel to drain.

STEP 5: Sprinkle the wildflower seeds on top of the wet pulp, patting them so they sink into the surface and seems like they will stay.

STEP 6: After the pulp has drained as much water as it can onto the towel, turn the hoop over and place the "paper" onto a sheet of waxed paper to dry. The paper will need about 24 hours to be completely dry and if it doesn't want to lie flat, you can put a towel over it again and place a heavy book on it for a few hours. Repeat until you have used up all of your pulp.

FAIRY HOUSE CRAFTS

his chapter assumes you've made a fairy house and are now ready to take it to the next level by creating furniture and accessories. It's really just a starting point, because once you get a handle on the techniques described in this chapter, there's no limit to what you can dream up to add to your fairy world. You might think of accessories that no one has thought of before.

Here are some projects to "feather your fairies nest." And as you work, keep in mind this question: What does a fairy house truly need for furniture? Think of how much stuff is inside your own house: tables, chairs, a couch, toys, beds, a bath tub, book shelves. The list goes on and on.

The Monhegan Rule

This is the biggest, most important, and maybe the only firm rule in fairy house building. If you are going to build a fairy house in nature, you must use natural materials.

One of the first places people began making fairy houses was a small island off the coast of Maine called Monhegan. The island is ten miles out to sea and has a very fragile ecosystem. People have to take a ferry to go see the fairy houses on Monhegan in a magical spot called Cathedral Woods. When people began building fairy houses they'd bring things they thought the fairies might like; glittering gems, tiny tea cups, coins, and other sparkly

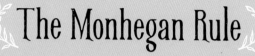

things. The shiny bits would attract animals who thought it was food. Sometimes animals would get sick, but most of the stuff would get thrown around during a Maine winter, becoming litter in the woods.

So one day, a woman who lived on the island decided to gather all this non-natural stuff and put it in a pile at the start of the trail to Cathedral Woods. The pile was huge! She made a sign telling people that from now on fairy houses could only be made with natural materials to protect the woods and the animals.

But here's the thing . . . if you're building a fairy house right outside your door and wild animals won't be confused into eating your sparkles, then it's okay to use a little non-natural thing every now and again to jazz up your house. And this is especially true if you are bringing your fairy house inside. But keep in mind, I've always felt that fairies would rather sit on a chair made of twigs than one made out of plastic.

The most important thing about making tiny twig furniture is that you need a plentiful source of twigs. And a steady supply of glue from a glue gun. (Note: I will say this over and over—always have an adult nearby when you are using a glue gun to avoid burns or other hot glue mishaps.) Most of the following twig furniture pieces rely on what authors and fairy artists, Mike and Debbie Schramer call the "twig square." This basic building block is simply four twigs glued together to make a square frame. This section covers essential pieces like chairs, tables, and beds, but twigs are also used in making ladders, fairy hammocks, and even fairy brooms.

{ Twig Chair }

The phrase, "pull up a seat" is one of the best ways to welcome someone into your home so making a chair to welcome a fairy into your house is guaranteed to warm the hearts of visiting fairies.

YOU WILL NEED

8 to 12 twigs about 1½ inches long

Glue gun

Birch bark or a small piece of bark cut into a square

Decorations like moss, dried flowers, seeds, tiny shells

INSTRUCTIONS

STEP 1: Take your four twigs and create a square for the seat of your chair. Glue each corner until you have all of them connected into what looks like a frame.

STEP 2: Glue a square of bark over the frame of your chair's seat.

STEP 3: Turn the seat over and hot glue each chair leg (smaller twigs) to each corner of the chair seat. Optional: You can create braces across your chair to make it more sturdy. There are a few ways to do this: one way is to add another twig across the center of two legs like the rung of a chair. Or you can create an x from two crossed sticks on two sides of your chair. Continue on all four sides.

STEP 4: Use a rectangular piece of bark or several small twigs to create the back of the chair. Decorate the chair with dried flowers, moss, and tendrils to make it look fanciful and ready for a fairy queen.

{ Twig Table }

No fairy home would be complete without a table so fairies can share a feast or a cup of tea. Setting a table with dishes and tea cups will most certainly welcome the fairies and allow them to replenish themselves after busy days of flying around. They might even set their tiny paper on this table to write to you about their adventures.

YOU WILL NEED

4 twigs about 2½ inches long for the table top frame

A piece of birch bark for table top or a tree round

Glue or glue gun

Moss and berries for decoration

INSTRUCTIONS

STEP 1: Create a larger "twig square" (similar to what you did with the chairs) by gluing the four even twigs together to create a frame. This will become the tabletop.

STEP 2: Place a square of bark over this frame a tree round, or lay a series of twigs equal in size in a row and glue each one to the outside of the frame.

STEP 3: Glue legs to your table as you did with the chairs.

STEP 3: You can add braces like you did for the chair by gluing cross twigs to connect the inside frames.

STEP 4: Decorate with moss or berries and then get ready to set the table!

{ Fairy Bed }

A fairy bed is one of the most essential accessories in a fairy house because, let's face it, fairies love to sleep and dream. This fairy bed gives the fairies a decorated headboard but it's just one example since there are no limits on how and what you can use to make a fairy bed. The only key is to make it soft and fluffy.

YOU WILL NEED

Flat piece of birch bark about 4 inches long and at least 3 inches high

Scissors

Tacky glue or glue gun

2 twigs 5 inches long

2 twigs 3 inches long

Any of the following to decorate the headboard: small dried berries, lentils, shells, dried flowers, rose petals, sea glass, mica

Moss, feathers, or other soft grasses and leaves for the inside of the bed

INSTRUCTIONS

STEP 1: Cut a semi-circle out of the bark.

STEP 2: Arrange a design onto the piece of bark using the berries, shells, lentils, etc. Use your glue gun to attach your design onto the bark. This will be the headboard for your bed.

STEP 3: Using your glue gun, create a frame. Place the two longer pieces on either side of the headboard and the shorter branches on the top and bottom.

STEP 4: Fill the frame with moss, leaves, or flower petals and your fairies will have a wonderful rest.

{ Twig Ladders }

Twig ladders are especially helpful for fairies to use as they climb deep into a giant pumpkin or high up on a tree trunk. Find two straight sticks that are about the thickness of your pinky and about six inches long. Take a skinnier twig and break it into about five pieces of equal length. Using a glue gun or strong white tacky glue, attach each rung of the ladder to the sides.

{ Fairy Hammock }

Who doesn't like to spend an afternoon reading and resting in a hammock? Making a fairy hammock gives the fairies another place to take their nap and it's a cinch to make!

YOU WILL NEED

1 4-inch twig

2 2-inch twigs

2 2½-inch twigs

A piece of cheesecloth or tulle about 8 inches long and 4 inches wide

2 twist ties or pipe cleaners cut in half

Glue

INSTRUCTIONS

STEP 1: Glue the each end of your 4-inch twig to the middle of a 2-inch twig to create an I shape. This is the hammock base.

STEP 2: Next, glue each 2½-inch twig so it is sticking up from the middle of each end of the I. These are the poles where the hammock will be attached.

STEP 3: Take the cheesecloth or tulle and squeeze each end together and wrap it with a twist tie or pipe cleaner. Then loop the remaining ends of the twist tie or pipe cleaner around the two twig poles.

STEP 4: You can make a tiny pillow for the hammock out of soft leaves, moss, or even sew one out of fabric so that the fairies can have even more comfort.

{ Fairy Broom }

airies are very tidy and they love having a broom at the ready for some clean up when things get too dirty. Making a fairy-size broom is pretty simple and the bristles can be made from a whole range of materials, such as feathers, pine needles, or evergreen branches.

YOU WILL NEED

A thin twig about 2 to 3 inches long

Feathers, pine needles, or evergreen twigs to use as bristles

Thin wire or a short pipe cleaner

INSTRUCTIONS

To attach the selected bristles, place the tips at the base of your stick, then wrap a small piece of pipe cleaner or thin wire around the tips of the feathers and the base of the stick many times so that it is secure.

{ Fireplace }

As the days get shorter and cooler, fairies appreciate a chance to sit by a crackling fire to warm their tiny toes. Even if it isn't an actual fire, maybe they can sprinkle a little fairy dust to light one up. This craft is one that falls in the backyard/indoor fairy house department as it uses cardboard. Although paper is a natural material, it turns into litter after a short time.

YOU WILL NEED

The bottom of a small gift box (about 4 x 6 inches)

Ruler

Pencil

Scissors or an X-Acto knife
(a grownup should do this part)

Glue

Pebbles
(if you don't have a good source of pebbles, most dollar stores and big box stores sell them)

INSTRUCTIONS

STEP 1: Use the ruler to mark a rectangle on the outside bottom edge of your box.

STEP 2: Ask an adult to cut this portion out of the box.

STEP 3: Cover the box with tacky glue and layer it with the pebbles. Wait a couple of hours for the glue to dry before trying to move the box. Then set it in your fairy house and fill with tiny logs.

OPTION: You can assemble a box shape out of bark and then cut out a small rectangle and glue on the pebbles for a natural alternative.

{ Sea Shell Sink }

As I mentioned before, fairies are tidy creatures, so having a sink for them to wash their hands in is a welcome treat. This simple project has many ways to expand. Are there other things you could use to make a sink bowl or a sink base? Let your imagination go wild with the possibilities.

YOU WILL NEED

Glue

A shell with a deep bowl

A thick, short twig for the base

A small tendril, very thin curly roots, or tiny twigs for the faucet

INSTRUCTIONS

Simply glue the end of a thick short twig onto the bottom of a shell . Cut the tendrils, roots, or twigs into two pieces and glue them to the shell to look like hot and cold faucets. You also can paint the shell and add beads to decorate the outer ring of the shell.

{ Rugs }

Putting a rug in a fairy house is another way to make it really cozy for the fairies. I love having a soft rug to rest on and cushion the hard floor. Making fairy rugs is also a very open-ended project. Some kids simply use big leaves like hosta leaves or softer ones like lamb's ear. My children were always partial to weaving small rugs out of long reeds and grass and their rugs would last through many seasons of fairy house building.

{ Fairy House Mailbox }

(Adapted from Fairy House *by Mike and Debbie Schramer)*

 aking a mailbox is a great way to communicate with the fairies when they visit your fairy house. Later on, we will make fairy mail boxes for your room, but why not have an outside and inside mailbox. Fairy mail is always the best mail.

YOU WILL NEED

Small piece of curled bark
> (Often cherry trees shed small curly bark that would serve as a perfect mailbox. If you can't find this, soaking a small piece of birch bark in warm water, will allow you to curl it.)

Thumbnail-size piece of bark for the mailbox door

Thick twig or a small piece of driftwood or a root for the mailbox stand

A few stones for the base of the mailbox

Red leaf or red petal (to be cut and used as the flag)

Glue gun

INSTRUCTIONS

STEP 1: Cut the thumbnail sized bark piece to fit on the opening of the curled bark. Glue it to the bottom of the opening so the mailbox stays open.

STEP 2: Glue the mailbox to the twig, driftwood, or root with your glue gun. Surround the base with stones so it stands upright. You can glue the stones to the base, if you like.

STEP 3: Cut the red leaf or petal into a flag shape and glue it on the side of the mailbox to let the fairy mail person know that the mail is here.

{ Leaf Envelopes }

Leaf envelopes are simple to make, elegant looking, and durable. The added bonus is the variety of leaf colors throughout the seasons. Adding the wax seal is a completely optional step and requires some parental help, but if you have a wax seal and some beeswax on hand, your leaf envelope will look pretty classy.

YOU WILL NEED

Scissors

A fresh leaf

Glue, (tacky glue or glue gun)

Optional: A wax seal and beeswax

INSTRUCTIONS

STEP 1: Cut a square shape out of the center of your leaf.

STEP 2: Fold two of the side corners in to meet each other. Seal with a drop off hot glue or tacky glue. If using tacky glue, press firmly so glue sticks. Then fold one other corner up to the center to meet the other corners and glue.

STEP 3: Now you will have your envelope. You can cut another square out of a leaf to write a message for the fairies. Place it inside your envelope and fold the last corner down. Seal either with a wax seal or a dot of glue.

There are two types of fairy umbrellas here: one is for fairies to have when it rains and one is for the garden to protect them from the sun when they are dining outside. Both rely on non-natural materials so are great for your fairy garden or indoor fairy house.

{ Personal Fairy Umbrella }

(Adapted from Kiwi Co Corner)

This simple project can add a bit of flourish to a fairy's flowery outfit and serve as their tiny parasol to keep their delicate skin from getting too much sun.

YOU WILL NEED

Fabric flowers

Wooden shish kebob skewers cut in half

A small ball of clay

INSTRUCTIONS

STEP 1: Pull all the fabric flowers off of their stem. A little hole will be in the center of the flower.

STEP 2: Choose a variety of flowers to layer onto the skewer. You can stick the skewer into a banana to hold it upright while you place your flowers on the stick.

STEP 3: When it is all set, have a grown up cut off the point on the skewer so it isn't pokey. Take the small ball of clay and slide it on the very top of the flowers so they don't fall off.

{ Garden Party Umbrella }

(Adapted from Fairy House *by Mike and Debbie Schramer}*

This umbrella is perfect for a picnic table or to set poolside to keep the fairies in the shade while they read or visit with friends. It takes a bit more time than the last project but the outcome is well worth it. You

WILL NEED

Pot pie container or paper bowl

Fabric flowers or dried flowers

Glue

A thin but sturdy twig

Clay for the base

INSTRUCTIONS

STEP 1: Paint the bowl a color that matches the flowers you are going to use. Let the paint dry before adhering the flowers. Trim the edges of the bowl or pie container to make it a more rounded shape.

STEP 2: Start to decorate the outside of the bowl with the flowers. Glue them close together to cover all the blank space on the pie plate.

STEP 3: Once the flowers have had a chance to dry, glue the twig umbrella stand to the center of the inside of the bowl. Hot glue will work best for this project. If the umbrella feels wobbly, you can brace the canopy by gluing four small twigs from the stand to the insides of the umbrella. Take a small ball of clay and roll it into a ball. Stick the umbrella into the clay and work the clay around the stand so it is completely supported. Add more clay as needed to give good support.

NOTE: For a simpler project like the one in the picture, you can substitute a cork for the pot pie container or paper bowl.

{ Rose Hip Tea Set }

This activity is dependent on perfectly ripe rose hips from a *Rosa Rugosa* bush. The rose hips need to be slightly soft to the touch but not too squishy. Rose hips are a brilliant red when they are ripe and can usually be harvested in late summer and early fall, just when the fairies will really need a cup of tea!

YOU WILL NEED

Rose hips of several sizes
> (The biggest can be made into a tea pot, mediums can be turned into a sugar bowl or a creamer, and small rose hips can become your tea cups)

Knife
> (parents need to help with this part)

Coffee stirrer or Popsicle stick

Stems from leaves

INSTRUCTIONS

STEP 1: Lay out your rose hips on a cutting board. With a grownup's help, use a small knife and gently cut a circle around the top of each rose hip. Be patient, because sometimes the rose hip will collapse and you will need to use a stronger one.

STEP 2: Once you have cut around the top, you are ready to scoop out the seeds. Wooden coffee stirrers or Popsicle sticks work well for this task. Again, patience is needed, as well as a gentle touch.

STEP 3: Now, you are ready to make the handles. Gather some leaves and cut off the stems. Cut off the little bumpy end of the stem where the leaf was attached to the branch. Look at your hollowed out rose hip and bend the stem to see how long you need to make the handle.

STEP 4: Pierce the end of the stem into the lower end of the rose hip, supporting the inside with your finger. Bend the stem and press into the upper part of the rose hip. This might take a few tries. Again, be patient. Now you can fill your cups with sweet juice or nectar for the fairies to enjoy.

{ Acorn Tea Set }

YOU WILL NEED

Acorn with cap attached

4 small acorn caps

Tendrils, thin curly roots, or very, very thin twigs

Glue

INSTRUCTIONS

STEP 1: Make the tea pot by taking the acorn and gluing on a handle made out of the thin twigs or tendrils. Glue a tiny berry or tiny shell to the very top of the acorn cap to decorate it.

STEP 2: Glue handles on the acorn cap cups and set around the tea pot.

Fairy Play Ground

Fairies love to play, so why not build them a playground? Swings, a see-saw, a slide, a sandbox, and monkey bars are all easy things to build with natural materials.

Swings can be made in a variety of ways. You can find a rectangular piece of bark and loop two pieces of twine around each side. Attach your swing to a frame made out of twigs. You could also use a piece of sea glass or a flat rock for the seat of your swing.

A see-saw can be made by balancing a piece of bark on a rock.

Sometimes, a slide already exists in nature. Look for smooth rocks that are at an angle or the base of a tree that has lost its bark. Otherwise, find a smooth piece of bark or a narrow, flat rock and lean it at an angle to create a slide. You can build a ladder for fairies to climb or assume they might fly up to the top of your slide!

Monkey bars can be made just as you would make a ladder by gluing rungs to two equal-sized twigs. Then make the supporting bars and stand them in the ground.

If you have a sand box or live close to a beach, borrow a cupful of sand and use twigs to outline a fairy sand box. Acorn caps are good pails for fairy sand castle building.

3

NATURAL FAIRY DOLLS

ometimes after making all of this amazing stuff for your fairy house, it's fun to make some fairy dolls to actually play in the house while you wait for real fairies to visit. Otherwise, how will you know if the chairs will fit or the bed is comfortable enough? These fairy dolls also make great gifts for fairy enthusiast friends.

{ Flower Fairy }

This simple flower fairy craft can be adapted all summer long according to the changes in your garden. Each flower will add its own personality to your fairy. Come up with names for them and maybe you can even write a story about your flower fairies as they change through the seasons. Try to be flexible and patient with this craft as it can sometimes take a few tries to get it just right.

YOU WILL NEED

A Y-shaped stick

A straight twig, about 2 to 3 inches long

Long grass or twine

Glue

A poppy pod, a bud, or flower
   (acorns or small pinecones work too but you will need to glue them on to the stick)

Petals for clothing

INSTRUCTIONS

STEP 1:   When turned upside down, the Y-shaped stick is your flower fairy's legs and the smaller stick is the arms. Make a cross with the two sticks with upside down Y on the bottom. Connect the cross with either a dab of glue or wrap a long piece of grass around the intersection to secure. This center point is the body of the fairy.

STEP 2:   The poppy pod or bud, or the center of a flower will be the fairy's head. Poke the top of the Y into this round piece. If you are using an acorn or a pinecone, you will need to glue it to your stick.

STEP 3:   Use any sort of a petal and tie it below the arms of your fairy with another piece of grass. This is the skirt for your fairy. You can add a hat by finding a pointed flower, such as a blue bell or a daylily.

{ Woodland Fairy }

t my daughter's school, they have an old tradition of going to a nearby nature center and creating what they call "Peeps." These are stick characters that use natural materials for clothing, hair, and accessories. It's amazing what some pine needle hair, berry eyes, and mossy skirts can do to a stick! And if you add some wings, they easily become fairy peeps. The only difference between these fairies and the flower fairies is that instead of flowers for clothing, you can use all kinds of woodland treasures to make this fairy more comfortable in the forest.

YOU WILL NEED

A Y-shaped stick, about 6 inches long

A straight twig, about 2 to 3 inches long

Long grass or twine

Glue

Collection of natural materials: moss, berries, mica, shells, acorn caps, bark

Wool roving for hair

INSTRUCTIONS

STEP 1: When turned upside down, the Y-shaped stick is your flower fairy's legs and the smaller stick is the arms. Using a piece of twine, lash the shorter stick in place across the body of your fairy.

STEP 2: Now gather lots of materials to make a head, clothes, eyes, a mouth, hair, a hat, and any other accessories that you can imagine. Using a glue gun or some tacky glue, attach your natural clothing so that your Peep won't be cold or, even worse, naked. Don't forget to add wings. Leaves work really well as do large flower petals.

STEP 3: You can also use a bit of clay to make a head for your woodland fairy. Clay has the advantage of being easy for stuff to stick to—such as pine needles for hair or pebbles for eyes—all touches that will make your stick fairy unique and life-like.

Fairy Clothing

Fairies love clothes. There are certain fairies whose only job is to make endless costumes. Try your hand at being a fairy seamstress. You can simply take a large petal and cut it with scissors. You can cut a hole in the center of a petal or a leaf to make a fairy poncho. A bigger hole will make it a fairy skirt. You can even put little berry buttons on your fairy fashions. Certain flowers make ideal fairy caps such as blue bells or hosta flowers. If your fairy house has an extra room, you might even need a closet for all of your clothing designs and definitely a laundry line filled with tiny clothespins.

{ Milkweed Pod Baby Fairy }

What could be cuter than a baby fairy? Perhaps a baby fairy wrapped in wool asleep in a milkweed pod. This is a very simple fairy craft that relies only on access to dried milkweed pods. If you don't have any milkweed nearby, plant some. It is one of the main ways that we are saving Monarch butterflies.

YOU WILL NEED

Wool roving

Acorn caps

Empty and dried milkweed pods

½ to ¾-inch round wooden bead

1½ to 2-inch very thin twig

Glue

Black fine point felt-tip pen

INSTRUCTIONS

STEP 1: Insert your twig into the hole of the wooden bead. You can add glue if it doesn't stay very well. This will be your baby fairy's body and head.

STEP 2: Wrap the twig with the wool roving so the body looks round and plump. Tuck the last of the wool into the folds or add a drop of glue so the roving doesn't unwind.

STEP 3: Glue the acorn cap on top of the baby fairy's head and then draw a mouth, eyes, and a nose on it.

STEP 4: Place your baby fairy in the milkweed pod so that it is nicely cradled.

{ Peg People Fairy }

here was a time when my daughters made hundreds of peg people fairy families. There was the willow family, the marigold family, the oak leaf family, and many more. We were completely outnumbered by peg people fairies! One of the things that furthered our enthusiasm around the peg people world was a delightful book called, *Making Peg Dolls* by Margaret Bloom. There is no end to the cool peg dolls you can make, but here is a simple peg doll fairy to start out.

YOU WILL NEED

Wooden peg dolls (found at most craft stores)

Felt, in a variety of colors

Paint and brushes

Fine point felt-tip pens in black and red

INSTRUCTIONS

STEP 1: Paint your peg doll's body in a fairy-ish color. Let dry for a few minutes and then paint on some hair. Use your fine-point marker to add eyes and a mouth to your fairy.

STEP 2: Make your fairy a pointed felt hat by cutting out a triangle piece of felt that has a very rounded edge. It should be 2 inches by 2 inches. Overlap the two straight sides to form a cone shape. Either glue the edges or sew them together and then glue onto your fairy's head. You can decorate this hat by gluing ribbon on the bottom edge or attaching a pompom or a small flower on the tip. You can also glue tiny beads around the edge.

STEP 3: Cut a small heart shape out of a different color of felt for the wings and glue them on the back of the fairy. Repeat until your fairy has enough friends to not feel lonely.

{ Straw Fairy }

(Adapted from Nature's Playground)

For centuries, people have been weaving straw from their harvests into doilies, knots, or fans. Many early farmers believed these woven straw creations would ensure a successful crop and they were often hung in the kitchen until the following harvest. To take a bunch of straw and transform it into a fairy-ish doll, you just need to add wings from a leaf or woven semi-circles.

YOU WILL NEED

Straw

Thin long grass

Raffia or twine

Scissors

INSTRUCTIONS

STEP 1: Make a bundle of straw and tie it together in the center using raffia, twine, or dried grass/straw.

STEP 2: Divide the lower half of the straw into two clumps and tie them with the twine or raffia. These are the legs and feet of the straw fairy.

STEP 3: Add arms by attaching a thinner bundle of straw with raffia at right angles to the fairy. Add wings by weaving in leaves to the back of your straw fairy.

{ Pine Cone Fairy }

(Adapted from Red Ted Art)

There is something very pleasing about seeing a plump pine cone with a head, wings, a hat, and hair. It's the ultimate woodland fairy doll. This pine cone fairy would make a great ornament for a tree or gifts for friends. The biggest challenge is how to make just one. So why not make an entire fairy fleet with different colored hair and wings?

YOU WILL NEED

Old tights

Stuffing

Thread or embroidery floss

Wool or yarn for hair

Acorn caps for hats

Felt for wings

Glue

A nicely-shaped pine cone, not too big

INSTRUCTIONS

STEP 1: First, make the head for the fairy by stuffing tights with a small handful of stuffing. Wrap the tights tightly around the stuffing to make a ball-shape. Tie the head together with thread or embroidery floss.

STEP 2: Cut some hair-colored yarn or wool roving. Glue it on the top of your fairy head with hot glue or tacky glue. Put glue inside the acorn cap and place it firmly over the fairy hair.

STEP 3: Bend the top few scales to flatten the top of your pinecone. Place a hearty dose of glue on this flattened spot and attach your fairy head.

STEP 4: Cut wing shapes out of the felt and glue wings in the center of the fairy's back. Let all the glue dry and make sure the head and wings stay in their right places. If you would like to make this an ornament, glue a loop of ribbon at the back "neck" of your fairy.

THE RECYCLED FAIRY HOUSE

Nothing is more important to a fairy than taking care of our planet and protecting the earth, although laughter is a close second. I'm sure you already know that one key way to help our environment is to recycle. So much of our trash is actually stuff that could have a second life, and what better life for a piece of trash headed to the landfill than to be claimed by you to make something for a fairy?

Perhaps you've read the delightful children's book, *The Borrowers*, by Mary Norton, in which a family of very tiny people live in the walls of an old house and create all of their essentials from bits and pieces they gather from the larger humans. If you look at the world like a character from that book, everything can magically take on another role. A sponge ready for the trash can become a couch cushion. Empty matchbooks can become dresser drawers. An empty spool can be a table. An old handkerchief can be curtains and a stray earring can be a chandelier. Look through your house and see what you can discover. Pull open that family junk drawer or dig through the recycling bin for odds and ends that can be transformed.

Speaking of transforming trash into treasure, two activities in this chapter (the Adobe Fairy House and the Translucent Home for a Light Fairy) were created by an artist named Robinsunne. She is a paper artist and an expert at turning leftover bits into magical creations. One of her favorite books is *The Borrower's* and part of why she enjoys creating these tiny houses for fairies is that she likes to imagine herself being that small and how cool it would be to live in the places that she creates. She also has fun taking care of and playing with the fairies who help her with her work. "It is good play time," she says.

{ Things to Save for Recycled } Fairy House Crafts

(Adapted from Dollhouse Magic*)*

This list is similar to the one in the beginning of the book, except it is compiled with the sole purpose of creating little worlds out of things found in your home. Keep an eye out for other things not on this list that might have a fairy purpose!

Beads

Small blocks

Boxes

Buttons

Birthday candles

Toothpaste caps

Charms from bracelets

Decorations from cakes and cupcakes

Party favors

Game pieces

Parts of jewelry

Lipstick covers

Lollipop sticks

Marbles

Nut shells

Empty spools of thread

Thimbles

Trimmings of lace

Old handkerchiefs and pieces of fabric

The Three R's

There are three very important R words that describe the things you need to do to take better care of our planet: Reduce, Recycle, and Reuse. We can't always do all three all the time, but we can get better at them with practice. For example, maybe you can make your school have a recycling program for straw wrappers, or perhaps you'll think twice about buying that little plastic ninja at the dollar store, or you might more happily wear your sister's hand-me downs. These are all ways to honor the three R's. But here are a few more ways that author Gwenn Diehn practices this vital earth-saving trio.

REDUCE: "I don't know about you, but I buy lots of things I don't need—like books I could get from the library or birthday cards or gift wrap I could make myself. When I can remember, before I buy something, I try to ask myself, Do I really need this?"

REUSING: "Reusing means saving something I might usually throw away and using it over again or giving it to someone else to use." Note: The crafts in this section rely on this principal!

RECYCLING: "Of course you know about recycling and why it's so important—mainly so we won't be buried under tons of garbage and make the air so polluted we can't breath. And also because not recycling wastes trees and energy and metal and oil and raccoons. Raccoons? Yes—every wild animal you've ever heard of. Because when we have to bury garbage . . . or when we cut down trees . . . or pollute the air by burning trash . . . we're messing around with the places wild animals live."

{ Robinsunne's Faux } Adobe Fairy Home

Have your parents ever bought a small appliance, like a lamp or a toaster oven, and you noticed the interesting shapes of the molded styrofoam packaging? I wished that I could live in a place like that, so I added a little texture, and a little paint, and now we have some very cool architecture for our tiny friends. Adobe is a type of house in the Southwest of the United States. It is made from sun-dried clay bricks and then coated with more clay to give it a nice smooth texture.

YOU WILL NEED

Molded foam packaging

White gesso or white acrylic primer

Paint brushes about 1" wide

1 to 3 acrylic artist tube paints in your choice of colors

1 to 2 big sheets of white tissue paper (more if your foam piece is big)

INSTRUCTIONS

STEP 1: Tear the tissue paper into 6-inch squares. Gently crumple each paper and then open them up again.

STEP 2: Paint a section of the foam with the gesso or primer. Squish a piece of the slightly wrinkly tissue paper on top of the gesso, and re-paint over the top of the tissue. Repeat all over the molded foam, front and back. If you have trouble getting the gesso and paper into any little crevices, don't worry: just make sure that the surface gets gesso-ed. Note: the tissue may rip, or bunch up. That is fine. It will just add a bit more texture.

STEP 3: Let this dry at least overnight. You could feed your fairies some supper and read them a couple of stories to pass the time.

STEP 4: When all the corners and crevices have dried, we get to paint. Sometimes I paint the whole house one color, and sometimes I paint certain sections a different color. You decide what is best for your fairy faux adobe home.

STEP 5: While the paint is drying, discuss with your tiny fairy friends whether they need any dishes or furniture in their home and help them make or gather those items. When the paint is dry (in about 24 hours) they can move in!

{ Robinsunne's Translucent } Home for a Light Fairy

This is a wonderful home for your fairy friends who need lots of air and light where they live. A quick note: this fairy house needs to be started the night before to prepare.

YOU WILL NEED

A clear, 2-liter seltzer bottle

Colored (pastel) tissue paper: big sheets of 2 or 3 colors that go together well

A base for the home: a piece of foam core, wooden plank, foam sheet, or even an old tray (you'll need an adult's help cutting it to the right size)

Strong scissors

Gesso or white acrylic primer

Gel medium or decoupage medium if it says that it works on plastic surfaces

1-inch craft paintbrush

INSTRUCTIONS

STEP 1: Cut the base to a good size for a fairy home landscape, and paint it with the gesso. Let it dry overnight.

STEP 2: Meanwhile, cut the bottom, bumpy section off of the bottle and cut out an arched doorway. Then tear or cut your tissue papers into 2-inch pieces, making separate piles of each color.

STEP 3: When everything is dry and ready, cover the top and sides of your base with one color of the tissue like this: paint a little area with gel medium and then place a piece of tissue on top. In order not to get sticky fingers use the paintbrush to push or brush the edges down. Keep gluing the tissue down, overlapping edges.

STEP 4: Decide where to place the bottle and glue it in place by painting a little gel medium on the lower outside rim of the bottle and a little more gel medium on the base. Then place half of a tissue square on the bottle and half on the base. Overlap these pieces and make your way around the bottom of the bottle.

STEP 5: Change colors of tissue paper whenever you want.

STEP 6: Keep working your way up toward the neck of the bottle. I like to leave a little bit uncovered to make sure that my fairies have lots of light. Let everything dry overnight and the fairies can take occupancy in the morning.

STEP 7: Decorate the neck of the bottle with short stems of flowers or chenille stems of stars, or a little string of beads.

{ Milk Carton Fairy House }

airies love milk. They give their babies milk baths and always welcome a sip as a treat. Chances are that you and your family probably go through a a lot of milk and rather than throwing away those cartons, why not transform them into a magical fairy house. This is a craft that is better for your indoor fairy world but you can decorate so it looks like it just came out of the woods.

YOU WILL NEED

A clean milk carton

Brown paint

X-Acto knife

Hot glue

Natural treasures like twigs, dried rose petals, mini pine cones, and pebbles

INSTRUCTIONS

STEP 1: Have a grown up help cut off the bottom of the milk carton and then outline where you would like windows and a door and have them cut those out too.

STEP 2: Paint the entire carton and set aside to dry for about half an hour.

STEP 3: Get your glue gun ready and glue on all of your natural treasures to make this fairy house come to life. Perhaps you can make a whole city out of old milk cartons for the fairies to live in!

{ Tiny Books for the Fairies }

nother great use for recycled paper is making tiny books for the fairies. You can even make a library for the fairies to visit. Making these books is very simple and you can make up your own titles or make miniature versions of your favorite books to share with the little people.

YOU WILL NEED

A few pieces of recycled paper

Scissors

Stapler

Fine-tipped markers or pictures from magazines to make the covers

INSTRUCTIONS

STEP 1: Cut a piece of the paper into a one-inch-thick strip that is about 10 inches long. If you want a really thick book like *Harry Potter*, you can make the strip even longer as the longer the strip the thicker the book will be.

STEP 2: Fold the strip of paper like an accordion and press the folded strip together so that you can staple one side.

STEP 3: Cut the other side so that the pages will be even and will turn.

STEP 4: Draw your cover or paste on a picture from a magazine. If you want to make a harder cover, you can wrap a piece of card stock around your book, cut it to the size of the pages and then staple it on.

{ Recycled Paper Origami }
Fairy Chair

lthough traditional origami masters do use special paper, there is no reason why you can't turn recycled paper into origami treasures. This way, you will be helping the earth and learning some the important lessons of origami, which include line of symmetry, geometric shapes, angles, area, measurement, making predictions, thinking spatially, and a whole host of other benefits. And even better, you can master these skills while making folded furniture for your fairies. I was lucky enough to be shown how to do this by some very talented 4th-grade origami enthusiasts. After you have mastered the chair, you can move on to a table and a bed. The magical and complex world of origami awaits! Note: If you are a visual learner, you might benefit from watching a video that explains this step by step.

YOU WILL NEED:

Recycled paper cut into a six-inch square

Popsicle stick to make your creases extra well-folded

Patience

INSTRUCTIONS

STEP 1: Fold six-inch square piece of paper in half and crease well with popsicle stick.

STEP 2: Fold the right and left sides so they meet at the middle crease, and then crease them well.

STEP 3: Fold the paper the other way, and crease.

STEP 4: Fold the top right corner to meet the first vertical line and crease.

STEP 5: Fold the left corner to meet the vertical line and crease.

STEP 6: Starting with the right corner, unfold the crease that you just created. Open it slightly and then squash it down to form a triangle. (This is a little tricky and takes some practice. You might also want to watch it on a video under "squash fold") Then do the same thing with the left corner.

STEP 7: Fold the center flap up to meet the top edge.

STEP 8: Fold the right side to the left and crease well then unfold. Then fold the left side to the right, crease and unfold.

STEP 9: Bring the top flap down. Tape or glue it so that it remains tight. Now you have a tiny chair made out of paper!

{ Fused Plastic Bag Rug }

There are way too many plastic bags out there and they take forever to go away. The best thing to combat the growing mountains of plastic bags, is to bring your own bags for shopping, but this activity is a great way to use up some of the bags that are just hanging around and turn them into something beautiful. Using this fused plastic technique, people have made amazing things like baby bibs, earrings, purses, bowls, and even rain coats. So consider this a starter lesson in a technique that can keep you crafting for years.

Important note: Fusing plastic involves heating and creates a very strong chemical smell. If you are sensitive to environmental smells or have a latex allergy, skip this craft. And this is definitely an activity where a grown up is needed.

YOU WILL NEED

An iron

Hard heat resistant surface (a wooden cutting board works well)

Ironing board

Baking parchment paper (not wax paper!)

3 plastic bags in a variety of colors

Scissors

INSTRUCTIONS

STEP 1: Cut off the handles and the bottom seam of all three bags to make nice rectangles. Keep the side seams connected so that you actually have two layers of plastic.

STEP 2: Put the iron on the synthetic setting and then open a window as ironing the plastic may release some fumes.

STEP 3: Cut two large pieces of parchment paper to sandwich the plastic. There will always be one piece of parchment on the bottom of the plastic and one on the top. You will fuse together one plastic bag at a time.

STEP 4: Now start to iron the top paper. Press firmly and keep the iron moving, don't let it sit in one spot for more than a second or two. After a few minutes, lift the paper to check your fused piece to see if has started to stick together. Rub it between your fingers and if you hear a crinkling noise then you need to iron it for longer.

STEP 5:   Now add the second bag on top of the fused plastic you just made. Put the parchment sandwich back together and iron for the same amount of time. Check it and then add the last layer.

STEP 6:   This is where you want to add your most colorful bag as this will be the top layer. You can also take small pieces of bright colored plastic bag and make a design on this layer.

STEP 7:   You will now have a large piece of fused plastic to make lots of rugs for your recycled fairy houses. You can cut it into all kinds of shapes.

5

FAIRY COSTUMES

o far you've collected things, created your own art supplies, built things for your fairy house, and made fairy houses out of things headed to the dump, so now it is time to become a fairy. Okay, maybe you can't actually be a real fairy, but you can certainly look and feel like one. All that a fairy needs is fairy wings, a beautiful skirt, special slippers, a wand, and maybe a necklace to hold fairy dust. This chapter has all of that and more. All of these costumes can be added to or changed to suit your particular color preferences or personal style, but once you've completed your costume there's another fun and optional step . . . creating a fairy play or dance recital. You can even make a stage and a set for your play and who knows, you just might catch the attention of the fairies since they love watching people play and dance.

{ Traditional Wire Wings }

(Adapted from kidspot.com.au)

These wings are a homemade version of the ones you most often see for sale at fairy stores and events. The wire component takes a bit of muscle but once you get that sorted out, these wings will really soar.

YOU WILL NEED

2 wire hangers

2 pairs of pink tights

Masking tape

Small piece of felt or scrap of fabric

Hot glue gun

Needle and thread

Optional extras: Glitter paint, fabric flowers, stick-on jewels and rhinestones

INSTRUCTIONS

STEP 1: Stretch one wire coat hanger so it forms a wing shape. Repeat with the other wire hanger and then place them on top of each other to check to make sure they are close in shape.

STEP 2: With the coat hanger hooks facing inward, twist each hook around the other to join your two wings together. You might need a little help with this as sometimes the wire is tricky to bend. You can even use pliers to make sure the hooks are wound tightly enough around each other so that no sharp ends stick out.

STEP 3: This wiry section in the middle isn't very nice to look at it so use a small piece of felt or scrap of fabric to cover it up. Wrap it around the wires and then seal it with masking tape so the wings have a nice padded spot that won't be pokey.

STEP 4: Cut both legs off a pair of tights. Stretch the tights over each hanger and gather the extra fabric in the center of the wings. Bunch that extra fabric

up in the center and wrap it around the felt square you just created. Tie it
in a knot and trim any extra fabric. Glue a fabric flower over this knot.

STEP 5:   The other pair of tights will serve as straps for your wings. Simply cut each
leg off and then sew each one to the backside of the center square making
two loops.

STEP 6:   The final step is to decorate the wings with jewels, fabric flowers, and
glitter gel.

{ Super-Easy Fabric Fairy Wings }

(Adapted from unhurriedhome.com)

ometimes you want your wings to feel light and breezy, and if so, fabric fairy wings are the perfect choice. These are also great for when you get invited to a fairy party and you can't find your other wings because you left them at fairy school. And like most crafts, you have complete control over what color you can choose for your wings.

YOU WILL NEED

1 35- x 35-inch square piece of silk or other gauzy, light-weight fabric
1 10- x10-inch square piece of silk or other gauzy, light-weight fabric
1 piece 50-inch long ribbon
2 pieces 20-inch long ribbon
ruler

INSTRUCTIONS

STEP 1: Tie two corners of the 10- x 10-inch piece of fabric together in a double knot.

STEP 2: Take the large piece of fabric and pull it half way through the hole and spread the fabric out. Tie a loose knot in the top two corners of the large square.

STEP 3: Thread the 20-inch pieces of ribbon through each of the two knots on the large piece of fabric, then tighten the knots so that they will not slip out. These ribbons are what you will tie on your wrists to make your wing's flutter.

STEP 5: Thread the large ribbon through the hole in the small square. This ribbon will go up over your shoulders, cross your chest, and then tie in the back.

NOTE: You can skip this last step and simply pin the wings to your shirt. Either way, your wings will be beautiful and fluttery and the whole thing only takes a few minutes.

{ Cardboard Wings }

I know this sounds less elegant than the prior two wings, but cardboard wings allow for a lot of creative flexibility. You can cover them in paint, fabric flowers, leaves, or create a papier mache effect with bright colors of tissue paper. They are great to make with friends and you don't have to feel like you need to keep them forever.

YOU WILL NEED

Large sheet of cardboard from an appliance
    box or other large box

Scissors

Pencil

Elastic

Hole punch

Decorating materials: leaves, tissue paper,
    paint, flower petals

INSTRUCTIONS

STEP 1:   Lay your cardboard on the ground and draw your wing with a pencil before you cut out the shape. Once you've decided on your wing design, carefully cut out the wings. Using a hole puncher, punch two sets of holes in the center top of the wings and the center bottom of the wings.

STEP 2:   Next comes the really fun part—decorating! Either paint a butterfly wing design or glue down layered flowers and leaves. If you want to create a tissue paper effect, tear or cut small squares of different colored tissue paper. Then using Mod Podge or watered-down glue, paint it over the tissue paper.

STEP 3:   Measure the length you will need your elastic to be to fit your arms and then cut it to length. Tie the elastic through the top hole on one wing and then loop it through the bottom hole with another knot. Repeat on the other side.

{ Fairy Tutu }

 nce you've created your wings, not having a tutu is like being naked in fairy terms. Luckily, fairy tutus are one of the easiest things to make for your fairy wardrobe and only require a quick trip to the fabric store.

YOU WILL NEED

Elastic

Scissors

Variety of ribbon colors

Tulle, either in one or a few colors

Fabric flowers

Hot glue gun

Optional: pom poms

INSTRUCTIONS

STEP 1: Measure the elastic around your waist and then cut it to length. Tie the ends in a double knot.

STEP 2: Cut long thin strips out of the tulle. Then simply knot the strips of tulle over the elastic, making sure they are an even length on both ends. Continue all the way around the elastic loop. Tie ribbons in the same way in alternating patterns around the skirt.

STEP 3: Hot glue fabric flowers all around the waist band to hide the knots. You can glue flowers on the skirt as well, or even pom poms if you choose.

That's it! Now you are ready to twirl!

Just like with wings, there are a million different types of wands to choose from, depending on the setting, mood, or type of fairy you want to attract. Here are some different versions: natural, cardboard, and really crafty. All of them will need to be powered up by your wishful thoughts before they can actually make magic. But I have no doubt they will be well fueled by your very creative imagination.

{ Nature Wand }

This is my favorite kind of wand. I think that sticks are automatically filled to the brim with magic and they are beautiful. The Nature Wand is extremely open-ended and can be changed to suit whatever materials you have on hand. The trick is in the very first step: finding the stick that you are magically drawn to.

YOU WILL NEED

A wand-length stick

Yarn in a variety of colors

Beads, cool charms, shells, bells

Ribbons

Paint or metallic spray paint

Paint brush

INSTRUCTIONS

STEP 1: If you would like to add some color, paint your stick first. You can spray paint with a metallic color to give it a sparkly undercoating.

STEP 2: After your wand is dry, wrap the top portion in varying colors of yarn. Once you have a nicely wrapped layer, begin adding your trinkets and beads. You can wrap wire around the objects without holes and then attach them to the yarn. Wrap ribbons around the very top of the wand and let them flow. The key is to fill the wand with vibrant color that will not only attract magic but the fairies themselves.

{ Painted Stripe Wand }

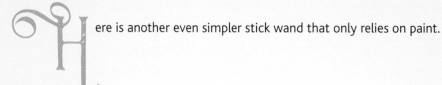

ere is another even simpler stick wand that only relies on paint.

YOU WILL NEED

Masking tape

Wand-sized stick

Paint

Brush

INSTRUCTIONS

STEP 1: Wrap your stick with several bands of masking tape. The bands can be close together or far apart. You can make a distinct pattern or keep it simple with random stripes.

STEP 2: Prepare your paint palette with a bunch of bright colors and then paint the stick different colors or patterns in between the masking tape. Wait for several hours before removing your tape, or at least until the paint feels dry to the touch.

STEP 3: Peel off your tape and reveal your colorful wand, all ready for magic and adventure!

{ Flower Wand }

This wand combines a little nature with the best of the craft world and works when you are appealing to the flower fairies. The goal is to create a wand that looks like it was created in a garden and is in full bloom. Surely magic exists wherever there are flowers, right?

YOU WILL NEED

Fabric flowers and dried flowers

Fabric leaves or fresh leaves

Raffia

Wand-sized stick

Hot glue gun

Tacky glue

INSTRUCTIONS

STEP 1: Find a wand-sized stick and gather a variety of fabric flowers and dried petals. Begin by hot gluing the blossoms on the top of the stick and covering as much of the top portion as looks balanced. One tip: if hot glue isn't working, you can cover your stick with colorful hair elastics looped tight and weave in the flowers so they are secure.

STEP 2: Cover the remaining part of the stick with leaves, dotting dried flowers along as well. Tie strings of raffia to drape off the top and glue fabric or dried flowers along these trails as well.

{ Star Wand }

This wand falls in the classic craft category. Cardboard, a little glitter, and a straight dowel. Because sometimes a very traditional and precise wand is needed to do your bidding and if so, this project is the one for you.

YOU WILL NEED

Cardboard

Pencil

Paint

Glitter

Dowel

Hot glue gun

White glue

Scissors

Ribbon

INSTRUCTIONS

STEP 1: Draw a star shape or a heart (or whatever shape calls to you) with pencil on the cardboard. Cut out your shape and then apply a base color of paint. Once the paint has dried, cover the surface with white glue and then let the glitter fly. Remember this is the classic sparkly wand so go all out, but make sure there is paper down so cleaning up isn't so challenging.

STEP 2: Hot glue the cardboard glitter bomb onto the dowel. Attach ribbons to the dowel to hang down or wrap the dowel completely in colorful ribbons. Bibitty boppity boo.

{ Fairy Slippers }

Just like Dorothy in *The Wizard of Oz* had her ruby slippers, for your fairy costume to be complete, you will need proper footwear. True fairy slippers are probably made out of bark, leaves, and fresh flowers. but this version allows for a more year-round and durable slipper. And once they are on your feet, who knows, clicking your heels might just to take you to fairyland! Also, this craft requires a pair of old shoes or slippers and thus, an adult's approval. Please whatever you do . . . don't take your best party shoes and transform them into fairy shoes.

YOU WILL NEED

Pair of old slippers, ballet shoes, or worn out party shoes

Hot glue gun

Green spray paint

Fabric flowers and leaves

Fake berries

INSTRUCTIONS

STEP 1: Paint the shoes with the green spray paint. Make sure to have a big newspaper down before spraying. Allow to dry for at least an hour.

STEP 2: Take one shoe and arrange a pattern with leaves, flowers, and berries. Make sure you have enough to repeat on the other shoe, unless you would like them to be different.

STEP 3: Use glue gun to attach the flowers, leaves, and berries to each shoe. Then slip those babies on and click your heels together!

Slippers for the Fairies

After seeing your amazing fairy slipper creations, what fairy wouldn't want their own pair? Luckily, making fairy slippers is a pretty manageable task due to their small size.

YOU WILL NEED

> Felt
>
> Thin cardboard
>
> Pencil
>
> Tiny paper flowers
>
> Small sequins and seed beads
>
> Glue
>
> Scissors

INSTRUCTIONS

STEP 1: Cut out two half-inch ovals out of cardboard and then cut one in half. This is your template for the slippers. Trace two ovals onto the felt and two half ovals. Cut each one out.

STEP 2: Glue the half oval around the edges onto the larger oval. Make sure there is a nice opening for a fairy foot.

STEP 3: Glue the tiny flowers, beads, and sequins onto the top of the slipper and then place them right by your fairy door.

{ Flower Crown }

There are tons of ways to make a flower crown. The simplest is to weave the stems of flowers through each other to make a daisy chain or dandelion crown. But you can also use pipe cleaners, ribbon, fabric, or grapevine wire to create the foundation for your crown.

So this one might take you by surprise but it's my favorite flower crown because as a bonus it utilizes recycled brown paper bags to help the earth.

YOU WILL NEED

A brown paper grocery bag

Scissors

Hot glue gun

Fabric flowers

Ribbon

Raffia

INSTRUCTIONS

STEP 1: First, cut off the bottom of the paper bag and begin rolling the bottom edges of the bag outward and upward, making sure to roll outward so the labels on the bag don't show through. Keep rolling the paper bag up all four sides carefully so that you avoid any rips. When you have rolled the entire bag, glue or tape down the loose edges so it creates a nice band shape. You might need to adjust it to fit your head at this point.

STEP 2: Wind the ribbon and raffia around your crown to help secure the shape. Then, using your glue gun, carefully attach your arrangement of fabric flowers all around the crown.

{ See-through Magic Crown }

The great thing about this crown is that because you use clear tape, it looks like all of the objects inside are actually floating around your head. Magic, right? But tape is sticky and so there can be an element of frustration when working with it. Just be patient and expect that the tape might get a little crinkled sometimes. This is an open-ended craft, so you can create any kind of color scheme or patterns. The only rule is that the objects need to be flat or else the tape won't seal.

YOU WILL NEED

Very wide clear tape, like packing tape

Scissors

Foil stars and sequins

Flat dried rose petals or other pressed flowers

Patterned paper

INSTRUCTIONS

STEP 1: Cut out shapes and strips of paper. Lay them in a line on a craft table. Cover them with the sequins, dried flowers, and other sparkles.

STEP 2: Place a length of clear tape (about a foot) over your decorated band of paper and sparkles and press firmly. Carefully peel the tape up.

STEP 3: Take another length of tape (the same length) and press over the sticky side so all of the stuff is sealed in tight. Repeat the process so you have enough length to wrap around your head. Staple the two sides together and then staple to size so it fits securely.

{ Toadstool Purse }

One problem with wearing fairy clothes is they don't have very good pockets. The easiest solution is to make a purse in the shape of one of the fairies favorite things—toadstools. I'm not exactly sure why toadstools are so beloved by fairies, but I do know they love to sit on them and watch the woodland world go by. This is a fairly easy sewing project which can be sewn by hand but if you aren't comfortable sewing, you can also just glue it together.

YOU WILL NEED RED FELT

Brown felt and red felt
White pom poms or white pony beads
Red grosgrain ribbon (2 feet long)
Scissors
Needle and thread (or glue gun)

INSTRUCTIONS

STEP 1: Cut out two 4- x 4-inch squares of brown felt. This is the base of the mushroom. Cut two half circles, 6 inches long on the flat side, out of the red felt.

STEP 2: Sew or glue the bottom of the red semi-circle onto the brown square, covering no more than an inch of brown felt, then repeat with the other one. Starting about halfway down one side of the outer edge of the red mushroom cap, sew the two mushroom sides together. Make sure you have a nice wide opening to put your fairy items into your purse. Sew on the ribbon right above where you connected the mushroom caps.

STEP 3: Glue the white pom poms over the red mushroom cap to make it look like a toadstool.

{Fairy Dust Pouch Necklace}

There's an old expression, "fake it until you make it," and this certainly holds true with fairy dust. It's pretty tricky to find real fairy dust because it's so valuable to the fairies. But there are some simple ways to make fairy dust and imbue it with your own special powers. I've included a couple of these recipes but when you are finished making your fairy dust, then you will need a special fairy dust necklace to carry it in. You can buy little corked bottles online and they are adorable, but you can also make a little cloth satchel that hooks onto a beaded necklace, similar to the leaf satchels fairies use to store their fairy dust.

YOU WILL NEED

4- x 4-inch square of fabric

Pinch of either of the following fairy dust recipes

Pipe cleaner

Beads

String

INSTRUCTIONS

STEP 1:   Take a pinch of your fairy dust and put it in the center of your piece of fabric.

STEP 2:   Fold all of the corners up so they meet each other and then twist it in the center so the fairy dust is securely in the pouch. Wrap the pipe cleaner around the center of the pouch several times.

STEP 3:   Wind the ends of the pipe cleaners together and form them into a hook.

STEP 4:   Bead a nice long, colorful necklace and then hook your satchel onto the middle of your necklace.

{ Good for the Earth } Fairy Dust

If you are lucky enough to have mica in your backyard or neighborhood, then this recipe can become a real staple. Otherwise, you can find mica online or if you travel to mountainous areas.

YOU WILL NEED

2 tablespoons ground up mica

1 cup sand or cornstarch

Mortar and pestle

INSTRUCTIONS

Basically, mica crumbles very easily and forms a very shiny, glittery powder. Mix one cup of playground sand or cornstarch with at least 2 tablespoons of mica. Add more mica to increase the shine.

{ Swirly Sparkly Fairy Dust }

YOU WILL NEED

Colored chalk

Various colors of glitter

Mortar and pestle

INSTRUCTIONS

Grind up your chalk with the mortar and pestle. Then mix in the glitter until you have a colorful sparkly fairy dust. You can add ground up flowers or herbs to make this into more of a potion.

YOUR FAIRY ROOM

Why leave all of the fairy fun in the backyard or keep your crafts in the living room or on the fridge? Why should the fun stop once you head to bed? Making your room a fairy oasis is a great combination of crafting and world building, otherwise known as interior decorating. Creating an enchanted fairy room will give you a magic space to dream about fairies, but it will also make a great pit stop for indoor fairies when they want a soft spot to lay their head or a refuge from the rain and cold. And remember, you can add all of these projects slowly because creating a magical room takes time.

There are several companies that make beautiful fairy doors to hang on your wall to welcome the fairies. It's great if you have one of these, but, I think it's even more fun to make your own version and customize it to make it just the way you want it to look. I think the fairies will truly appreciate coming through a door that was lovingly made by you and filled with that extra special creative power.

There are several ways to make a fairy door and I have provided four choices. Depending on what materials you have on hand or what you are most attracted to, you can choose one or make them all. Fairy doors also make great gifts for fairy-loving friends. You can add string to the back of any of these doors so you can hang them on the wall. Tape each side of the string to create a hook. This way you can play around with different locations to see what the fairies like best.

{ Natural Fairy Door }

This fairy door is one you can put in your outside fairy house or hang on your wall. And since it comes 100% from nature it will be a nice sight for fairies.

YOU WILL NEED

A nice flat piece of birch bark

Glue

Scissors

Lentils, acorn caps, moss, tiny shells, dried flowers

INSTRUCTIONS

STEP 1: Cut the birch bark with scissors into either a plain rectangle or an arched door. You might need help since bark can be a little tough and awkward to cut through. Then cut a window in the door. An X-Acto knife works well, too, but you'll need to ask a grownup to help.

STEP 2: Glue on your decorations gathered from nature. Remember to have a door knob so fairies can open the door and come on in.

{ Popsicle Stick Fairy Door }

Popsicle sticks are valuable currency in craft closets not to mention those uneaten popsicles in the freezer. Perhaps you've made log cabins, ornaments, or picture frames with popsicle sticks; well now it's time for a fairy door. This simple door gives a log cabin feel, sure to welcome fairies from out on the range.

YOU WILL NEED

7 (at least) Popsicle sticks

Glue

Watercolors or paint

Assorted decorations: buttons, moss, twine, bits of old jewelry, tiny shells or bits of sea glass

INSTRUCTIONS

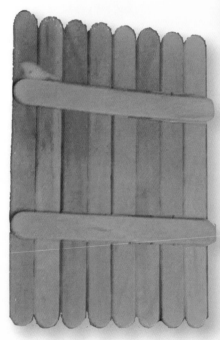

STEP 1: Place popsicle sticks next to each other. Usually five or six make a good width for a fairy door, but you can add more if you like.

STEP 2: Cut two other popsicle sticks in half to serve as the cross pieces to hold the door together. Glue these cross sticks over the other popsicle sticks.

STEP 3: After the glue dries, paint your door with either regular paint or watercolor to make it look more like a wood stain. Once the paint dries, glue your your treasures to your door to invite a fairy to step inside.

{ Extra Crafty Fairy Door }

his is the door where you can unleash your inner craft genius. Pull out those stickers, washi tape, and sparkly papers. Do you have leftover doilies from Valentine's Day? Stick them on. Wrapping paper from your birthday party? Why not? This is a great craft for a fairy party or when you have a bunch of friends over. And as is always the case, everyone's door will be completely different!

YOU WILL NEED

Cardboard

Washi tape in several varieties

Aluminum foil cut in a circle for a window

Stickers (flower shapes and insects work well but sky is the limit)

Decorative papers, doilies, wrapping paper

Metal brads for the door knob

OPTIONAL: If you have a source for adhesive moss strips, it adds a nice fairy element to the bottom of the door, but loose moss can be used as well.

INSTRUCTIONS

STEP 1: Cut an arched door shape out of the cardboard and then wrap it completely with washi tape. You can either use one pattern or several, but make sure the whole door is covered.

STEP 2: Poke your brad through the door (be careful) to serve as a doorknob. Glue on your aluminum foil window and then let the accessorizing begin.

{ Realistic Clay Fairy Door }

his fairy door is perhaps the most realistic and really resembles a true
elfin or gnome door. It probably takes the most time but will endure for
a long time. Not to mention how authentic looking it is. My guess is the
fairies won't be able to resist knocking on this one.

YOU WILL NEED

White Sculpey clay

A small and interesting button to serve as the doorknob

Acrylic paint in two shades of brown, light and dark (or you can just make
light brown by adding white to the dark brown)

Butter knife with a nice flat edge

Rolling pin covered in Saran wrap

Parchment paper

INSTRUCTIONS

STEP 1: Roll the white Sculptey into a golfball-size ball to warm it up and soften it,
then use the rolling pin to make it completely flat.

STEP 2: With your butter knife, outline the shape or your door in the clay and then
cut out your door. Using the blunt side of the butter knife, create lines in
the door to look like wood planks. Insert your button doorknob into
the clay.

STEP 3: Place the door on parchment paper and then prepare to bake it in the oven
according to the Sculpey baking directions. (Usually 10 minutes at 200
degrees.) Let it cool completely before beginning to paint.

STEP 4: Paint the whole door with the light brown and then while the lighter color
is still wet, add streaks of the darker brown to make it look like wood grain.
The two colors will blend and create an old weathered wood look.

{ Fairy Sleepover Bag }

Who doesn't love a sleepover? Setting this miniature sleeping bag and pillow out for a fairy will let them know they are always welcome to spend a night or three in your room. And you can even match the fabrics with your room décor to highlight your inner interior decorator.

YOU WILL NEED

4 fabric squares of contrasting but matching fabrics cut into 5- x 7-inch squares

2 fabric squares cut into 2- x 2-inch squares

Scissors

Needle and thread or a sewing machine

Stuffing for the pillow and mattress

INSTRUCTIONS

STEP 1:   Place two of the 5- x 7-inch squares together, one on top of the other, and sew three of the sides leaving an opening at the top. Turn the sewn square inside out. This will be the top of your sleeping bag. Sew the top seam.

STEP 2:   Repeat this step with the second set of squares, but after turning the square inside out, fill it with a flat layer of stuffing. This will the bottom, sleeping pad for your fairies. Sew the top seam.

STEP 3:   Now, sew these two pieces together along the outside edges and the bottom, but leave the top un-sewn and an inch on either of the sides so that you can fold over the top of the sleeping bag to make it look inviting.

STEP 4:   Place the 2-inch squares so that the backs are together and sew the outside edge leaving a small opening. Turn the fabric inside out and stuff with a small amount of stuffing, then sew the opening so you have a complete pillow. If you want to get really fancy, you can stuff the pillow with herbs like lavender or chamomile to help fairies sleep.

{ Leaf-Shaped Sleepover Bag }

This is a little less comfy for the fairies but might remind them of the forest that they love. It's also a good one when you don't feel like sewing and just need a quick rucksack (another word for sleeping bag) for an impromptu fairy sleepover.

YOU WILL NEED

Green felt

Hot glue

Scissors

Dark green marker

INSTRUCTIONS

STEP 1: Using a washable marker, draw a leaf shape on your green felt. It should be about 5 inches long to make it easy enough to work with. Cut it out and then trace it onto more green felt to cut out a match.

STEP 2: With your glue gun, carefully trace glue around the bottom half of your leaf and then place the top leaf on top. There should be a nice place for a fairy to slide in to take a nap.

STEP 3: With a dark green marker, draw the skeleton of a leaf on both sides of the sleeping bag.

{ Indoor Fairy Mailbox }

(Adapted from Red Ted Art}

Have you always wanted to be pen pals with a fairy? Apparently they really like to write tiny letters and keep up with their child friends. And writing the words, "Dear Fairy" has a magical ring to it, doesn't it? But the fairies need a way to reach you with their important messages so the following craft is a simple way to make an indoor mailbox to let the fairies know the mail's here.

YOU WILL NEED

1 empty matchbox (Note: Matchboxes are harder to find these days but can sometimes be found at Dollar Stores complete with the matches. You can buy craft matchboxes online which are empty and white but cost a little more.)

Red paint

Paper

Black permanent marker

Glue stick

X-Acto knife

INSTRUCTIONS

STEP 1: There is something classic about a red mail box, but you can paint it any color you like. Make sure to paint the inside of the box, too, so it will look pretty when you pull it out to check for mail.

STEP 2: Once the paint has dried, take a tiny piece of white paper and cut it into a square. Write "Mail Box" or "Fairy Mail" or whatever you want to say with a black pen and then glue the sign to the matchbox. Use the black pen to outline where you would like your mail slot to be.

STEP 3: Have an adult cut out a rectangular opening in the box to serve as the mail slot. It can be a little tricky so they may need to go slowly and cut carefully. That's it! Now wait for the fairy postal worker to make their first delivery.

{ Tiny Envelopes }

Now that you have a mailbox, you might want to have a stash of tiny envelopes ready for your fairy letter writing. Making tiny envelopes is very simple and fun. Once you master the tiny envelope, you can use the same process to make your own larger-sized envelopes for writing to bigger people.

YOU WILL NEED

3- x 3-inch square piece of craft paper

Glue

Pencil

INSTRUCTIONS

STEP 1: Mark a dot on the center of the square. Fold any two opposite corners equally towards the center. Both corners should meet each other in the center.

STEP 2: Fold the bottom corner up to meet in the center. You will have a corner of the triangle poking out.

STEP 3: Take that little corner and fold it under the two other pieces. Then stick a bit of glue to hold it all together. Now you will have a little pocket.

STEP 4: When you have filled your envelope with your magical letter, fold the top down and stick a little sticker or sticky gem to seal your note or wish!

{ Fairy Canopy }

Sleeping in a bed with a fairy canopy is certain to give you good dreams and perhaps even a nighttime glimpse into the fairy realm. It's a beautiful addition to any room, especially one with a fairy theme. And the best part is that it's really easy to make and not very expensive. Hanging this up is a bit of a commitment, so make sure to okay it with your parents before you get too attached to the idea.

YOU WILL NEED

Small hula hoop

5 spools of ribbon

10 to 12 yards of tulle

Fabric glue

Decorations: fabric flowers and butterflies (and any other fairy-ish thing)

Hook for hanging canopy

Measuring tape

INSTRUCTIONS

STEP 1: Wrap ribbon completely around the hula hoop to cover the plastic.

STEP 2: Cut the tulle into 6- to 8-foot lengths. (You will need a big space to do this as the fabric needs to be spread out to cut and measure).

STEP 3: Knot the tulle around the hula hoop. Tie more ribbons to the hula hoop and let them drape down over the tulle.

STEP 4: Using fabric glue, glue on the flowers, butterflies, and whatever else you have to make this canopy magical.

STEP 5: Tie four pieces of ribbon that are at least 2 feet long at four equidistant points around the sides of the hula hoop. Tie them together in a knot.

STEP 6: Have an adult screw a hook in the ceiling over the place where your head rests on your pillow. Hang the canopy from the knot on the ribbon. Spread out the bottom of the canopy so that it completely covers your bed. Sweet dreams!

{ Fairy Flower Curtain }

This petal and beaded curtain gives your room a certain disco quality and the colorful flowers and beads will brighten your room all year long so it feels like an indoor garden. There are lots of ways to adapt this curtain by varying the flowers you choose and not using drinking straws but instead choosing to use longer beads in their place. Basically, all you need to do is to thread long strings of beads and flowers to create a curtain effect.

YOU WILL NEED

Ruler

Scissors

Strong thread

Colored plastic beads

Large yarn needle to make threading easier

Plastic drinking straws (not clear)

Fabric flowers

Wooden rod 2 to 3 feet long

INSTRUCTIONS

STEP 1:   Cut the thread so it is twice as long as the length you want your curtain to be. If you want it to hang in a door, measure the distance from top to bottom; and if it is just going to be in a window, do the same thing.

STEP 2:   Cut the drinking straws into 2-inch sections. Then pull apart your fabric flowers so they come off of the stem. When you pop the flowers off, they will have a small hole in the center.

STEP 3:   Arrange your pattern or just begin stringing together your beads, straws, and flowers.

STEP 4:   Repeat 4 or 5 more times depending on how wide you would like your curtain to be.

STEP 5:   Tie each string to the wooden rod with at least 4 inches between each string. To hang the curtain, either hammer in two nails to either side of your window, door, or wall, then rest the rod on top of the nails; or attach another piece string (length twice as long as rod) and tie it at each end of the rod. Hang the curtain in the center of this string by a nail.

As an alternative to the beaded flower curtain, you can also make this into a mobile by simply taking two same-size sticks or rods and connecting them in the center to form an X. Tie your strings on each of the four corners for a shimmering mobile.

{ Painted Flags }

I f you want to make a place look festive, adding a colorful garland is a great way to start. There are tons of different ways to make garlands including using paper or fabric. You can choose one or several of them for a fairy carnival feel.

YOU WILL NEED

Paper

Paint and paint brushes

Scissors

Glue

String

Pencil

INSTRUCTIONS

STEP 1:   On a piece of cardboard, cut out a triangle that is at least one foot long from the top point down to the flat bottom (you'll actually hang the triangle upside down). Cut out 10 triangles. Lay them on a tarp or the lawn. Dip your paintbrush into one of the colors and then flick it across the triangles to create a splatter effect. Continue with more colors and make sure all triangles are covered with paint.

STEP 2:   When the splatters have dried, glue the flat edge of the flag and fold it over the string you have prepared for the garland. Press the edges down to create a seam. Continue with the other triangles until you have a full garland.

{ Flower Paper Garland }

YOU WILL NEED

- Paper
- String
- Scissors

INSTRUCTIONS

Cut out a series of flower shapes and leaf shapes, at least ten of each. Glue the tops of the flowers and leaves and fold the top edge over the string. Press the edge down until you have a seam. Continue until you have glued on all of the flowers and have a full garland.

{ Tissue Paper Banner }

YOU WILL NEED

Various Colors of tissue paper

Scissors

Glue

String

INSTRUCTIONS

STEP 1: Cut your tissue paper into rectangles that measure 10 x 6 inches. Fold each tissue rectangle several times and cut out shapes just like when making paper snowflakes. Unfold the rectangles and press under a heavy book until the folded lines begin to disappear.

STEP 2: Put glue along the top of the rectangle and fold over the string. Continue with the remaining rectangle flags.

{ Fabric Bunting }

This traditional bunting is a long-lasting and festive addition to your room. You can use the same fabrics that you used for your fairy sleepover bag to keep the colors coordinated, and you can even make a miniature one for your fairy garden to match.

YOU WILL NEED

Fabric in a variety of patterns

Scissors

Cardboard triangle template

Marker

A sewing machine or needle and thread or glue

INSTRUCTIONS

STEP 1:   You can use the same template from the painted flag craft or make another cardboard triangle as a pattern. Place the template on the different fabrics and trace triangles with the marker. Cut out about ten different triangles.

STEP 2:   Fold the fabric over the string but this time, run the top through a sewing machine or sew by hand so the flag is attached. If you are short on time, you can also use glue.

STEP3:   Continue until all flags are attached and then hang the bunting up in your room. Remember to make a matching tiny version for the fairies!

{ Fairy Lantern }

Are fairies afraid of the dark? Probably not, but just in case, you can have this lovely fairy lantern, also known as a fairy nightlight holder, on hand to soothe any jitters. And, as is the case with most of these crafts, you don't need to just make one. Your room would look pretty magical with lanterns strung though out to light up the night.

YOU WILL NEED

A small clean jelly jar

2 pieces of 1-foot-long thin wire or pipe cleaner

A variety of interesting beads

LED tea light

INSTRUCTIONS

STEP 1: Thread beads onto the pipe cleaner or wire.

STEP 2: Wrap the beaded wire tightly around the rim of the jar and clamp the ends tightly so it is nice and secure.

STEP 3: Make a beaded lantern handle by taking the wire and putting a couple of beads on either end. Twist the ends so the beads don't slip off. Loop each end into the wire that you have already wrapped around the jar and bend to form a handle shape.

STEP 4: Place your LED light in the bottom of the jar and turn it on when night falls.

{ Fairy Teepee }

A teepee can be simple or complex, plain or decorated. But a fairy teepee . . . well, that's just a dreamy oasis. This teepee is covered in twinkling lights and makes a great spot to read about fairies, write fairy tales, and draw fairies. This is definitely a project that takes many hands and probably a couple pairs of grown up hands as well. Not to mention, patience. This craft is intended for the outdoors, but if your room is big enough, you could certainly build one indoors too.

YOU WILL NEED

5 long sticks (6 feet long and 2 to 3 inches thick)

White sheer curtain or tulle or sheet

LED Christmas lights

Wire or string to tie top of teepee together

INSTRUCTIONS

STEP 1: You'll need to gather five long, straight sticks from the woods, a brush pile, or buy poles from a lumber center. Bamboo poles also work really well. Whatever you find, you'll need to cut them to be about 6 feet long and 2 to 3 inches thick.

STEP 2: Lash three poles together with the narrower ends at the top, tying them together with your wire or string. Do this while the poles are lying on the floor. Then lift them up, spread out the poles, and set the wider ends opposite the lashing in the ground, so they begin to resemble a pyramid or cone. Continue to add in the two other poles to give the tepee extra support.

STEP 3: Wrap the LED lights throughout the poles so they are evenly arranged. You can plug them in at this point to make sure there aren't any bald spots.

STEP 4: Now cover the teepee with your curtain or tulle. Tuck the top of the fabric into the wire or twine that you used to tie the sticks together. Make sure to leave a good opening for a door. Fill the inside of the teepee with cushions and blankets, bring in a good book and snuggle in.

7

FAIRY GIFTS INSPIRED
BY NATURE

o you endlessly scan the beach for interesting rocks, shells, and sea glass? When you come home from a walk, are your pockets bulging with rocks and other treasures? Is your night table or dresser top covered with endless natural wonders scoured from all of your adventures? On our family walks, I often get scolded by my family because it's hard for me to stop collecting acorn caps for fairy houses. I'm an avid sea glass collector, a rock hound, and am always on the lookout for oddly shaped sticks or big swaths of fallen bark. But after a while these piles of found objects really start to, well, pile up. Nature crafts not only make good use of these collections but they connect you to the beauty of nature. And what better thing to do with natural collections than make them into gifts.

It bears repeating that fairies love kindness. It's one of their essential purposes to highlight good things and encourage people to take care of the world around them. Making gifts inspired by nature is not only a way to make people happy but it will make the fairies immensely proud too.

{ Nature Print Wrapping Paper }

f you are gearing up for gift making, it's always good to have a stash of wrapping paper on hand. This wrapping paper made with nature as your paint brush will help your present stand out even more.

YOU WILL NEED

Evergreen branches, dried reeds, dried flowers

Newspaper to protect painting surface

Tissue paper

Paint

Paintbrush

Tray, old plate, or pie pan for spreading paint in

Cup of water

INSTRUCTIONS

STEP 1: Cover your table or workspace with newspaper to prevent paint spillage and splatters. Place a single piece of tissue paper over the newspaper.

STEP 2: Spread one color of paint on the tray or plate. Using the paint brush, spread the paint so it covers the bottom of the plate. Take the evergreen branch or whatever you want to use to make prints, and press it firmly into the paint. Place the object paint side down on the tissue paper and then press it down with newspaper so you don't get your hands too dirty.

STEP 3: Peel up the newspaper and the object and cover it with more paint. Repeat the process until the tissue paper is nicely decorated. Continue with other colors and plant choices until you have several sheets of wrapping paper.

STEP 4: Let the paper dry for at least an hour before using to wrap gifts.

{ Flower & Leaf Press }

A great technique for preserving various plant specimens is to make your own leaf press. It is a very simple project, as you are basically creating a squeezing machine. Once you have made this device, you can create lovely gifts out of dried and pressed flowers, including bookmarks, picture frames, and even jewelry.

YOU WILL NEED

Thick cardboard

Wax paper

Plant specimens

Rubber bands

INSTRUCTIONS

STEP 1:   Cut two squares of cardboard roughly one foot by one foot, then cut ten sheets of wax paper to be a little smaller than the cardboard.

STEP 2:   Place the plants you have collected in between two sheets of wax paper. Continue until you have placed all of your materials between the wax paper, but be careful not to overlap them.

STEP 3:   Sandwich your plant-filled papers between the two pieces of cardboard and then wrap it with loads of rubber bands so that you get a good squeeze effect.

STEP 4:   Wait several weeks before uncovering your plants. When you remove the rubber bands, you should have nice, flat plants and flowers to use in your journal or art projects.

{ Flower Perfume }

Nature is filled to the brim with beautiful scents and there are no better perfumes than the ones that come directly from flowers. Perfume is always a classic gift, so creating any of the following that rely on the divine scents from your garden will make a winning present with the added benefit of making your friends smell even better.

One way to capture the beautiful scents of summer is to make your very own flower perfume. Although it's not very hard to do, it does require some boiling water so a grown up should be nearby to lend a hand.

YOU WILL NEED

Cheesecloth

Flowers

Large pot

Water

INSTRUCTIONS

STEP 1: Gather the most fragrant flowers in your garden. You will need at least 2 cups of flowers.

STEP 2: Place cheesecloth over a sturdy pot. Place your flower collection on top of the cheesecloth and cover with water, making sure the cloth dips down into the pot and the flowers are covered in water. Let the flowers sit over night and through the next day.

STEP 3: Gather the cheesecloth with the flowers inside into a bundle and squeeze any extra water out into the pot of water.

STEP 4: Put the pot of flower water over medium heat and let the water boil until you only have a few teaspoons left. This will be your perfume! Pour it very carefully into a small glass jar and save for very special occasions.

Some perfumes to try:

PINE: To awaken the fairies

LAVENDER: To calm the fairies

PEONIES: To allow to dream of fairies

{ Bath Bags }

An even simpler way to capture the fragrance of flowers is to make bath bags as gifts. This uses the same technique that we used to make our fairy dust pouches, but instead of glittering magic dust, you will fill your pouch with dried herbs and flowers.

YOU WILL NEED

Pieces of muslin or cheesecloth cut in 4- x by 4-inch squares

Yarn, twine, or ribbon

Dried herbs and flowers

INSTRUCTIONS

This is very simple! Place a handful of dried herbs in the middle of the fabric. Bring the four corners together and squeeze the middle. Tie the bundle with ribbon or yarn and that's it. Your simple bath bag is ready to go for people's bathing pleasure. You can also create little tags to let people know what concoction you have created and that they just need to submerge the entire pouch in the bath.

{ Lavender & Rose Petal Sachets }

Who can't use a little help keeping underwear and sock drawers smelling fresh and clean? Sachets make great gifts for your teacher or a neighbor. You can sew these by hand or use a sewing machine, whichever you feel more comfortable with. The key is to pick really pretty fabric so that the sachet looks extra special.

YOU WILL NEED

Special fabric, either silk or patterned

Dried lavender and rose petals

Needle and thread or a sewing machine

Scissors

INSTRUCTIONS

STEP 1: Cut two 4- x 4-inch squares of fabric. Place the front sides together and sew three sides of the square. (If you would like to make your sachet heart-shaped, circle-shaped or any other shape you would like, go ahead!)

STEP 2: Turn your square inside out, so now the front sides are on the outside. Fill this pouch with the dried lavender and rose petals. Pin the top sides together and carefully stitch it together so the herbs don't spill out.

Here are some good herb combinations for a medicinal bath time experience.

PEPPERMINT & THYME are good when you have a cold.

PEPPERMINT & ROSEMARY give you energy.

LAVENDER & CHAMOMILE are good for relaxation and help you sleep better.

ROSEMARY & MARJORAM are good for tired muscles.

CALENDULA (MARIGOLDS) are good to soothe the skin.

{ Sea Shell Candles }

(Adapted from Nature Smart)

The beauty of these candles is that when you light them in the dark of winter, they will remind you of summer days at the beach. Some of you might not have easy access to shell collecting, and if so, no worries. You can almost always find shells for sale in stores all year long, no matter if you live by the ocean or inland. Making candles is an activity that definitely needs close supervision and help from adults. Hot wax is seriously hot stuff.

YOU WILL NEED

Newspaper

Large tin can (large canned tomato cans work well)

Medium-sized saucepan

Several lumps of beeswax, or bits and pieces of old candles
    (make sure there is no wick in them though)

Broken, old crayons

Pot holders

Several large sea shells

Small birthday candles (ideally the same
    color as the crayons used to color
    the candle)

Scissors

INSTRUCTIONS

STEP 1: Fill the saucepan halfway with water. Put the wax in the tin can and then place it in the center of the pot. Turn the heat to medium. If you want to add color, put the crayons in at this point.

STEP 2: As the water boils and the wax melts, prepare your shells. Put the news paper over the counter and set the shells up with rolled up paper towels to support them so they don't tip over while you pour the wax.

STEP 3: Have an adult pour the wax into the shells. Let them cool for about five minutes. They will look a little frosty on the top as the cooling process occurs. Cut a birthday candle in half and poke it into the center of the wax. This is your wick. Let the candle cool completely before lighting it.

{ Sea Glass Necklace }

I have a real love for sea glass and collect it whenever I take a walk on the beach. After the sea has polished and smoothed bottle glass, the sea glass really does come out looking like a jewel. Making sea glass jewelry is not only a great way to utilize a collection of sea glass, but it makes a very special gift. There is an option to use jewelry bails, which are tiny clamps that you glue on to the sea glass, but for a simpler jewelry experience, wire wrapped around sea glass works really well too.

YOU WILL NEED

Sea glass
Jewelry bails (clamps) or wire
Cord
Hot glue or special jewelry cement
Scissors

INSTRUCTIONS

STEP 1:   Lay out your sea glass to get a good sense of the different pieces you have in your collection. Arrange them according to color and size. With your hot glue gun, you can glue two or three pieces together to make an interesting stack. Either glue a pin-back or jewelry bail to the sea glass. If you are using wire, wrap the wire around your sea glass so that it is cradled in the wire.

STEP 2:   To make a necklace, string your cord through the jewelry bail or through the wire.

{ Birch Bark Pins }

irch bark, like sea glass, also makes beautiful jewelry. And because it is relatively easy to cut bark, you can create all kinds of shapes for pins. Adding a little sparkle or fabric jazzes it all up and makes for a show stopping piece. The trick is to use Mod Podge or watered-down white glue to make all of these extras shine.

YOU WILL NEED

Flat birch bark

Scissors

Mod Podge or white glue with water in it

Fabric, ribbon, buttons, paper flowers, or sparkles

Paint brush

Hot glue

Pin-backs

INSTRUCTIONS

STEP 1: Cut out a heart shape, flower shape, or whatever shape you feel like creating.

STEP 2: Place small cutouts of fabric, paper flowers, and whatever other decorations you are using in a pleasing arrangement on the birch bark shape. Dip your brush into the Mod Podge and carefully paste everything into place. Put a thick coating of the glue over it all at the very end.

STEP 3: With the hot glue, glue on the pin-back. Let the whole thing dry for several hours.

{ Sea Shell Wind Chime }

(Adapted from Nature Smart)

This sea shell wind chime is another solution for taming a large collection of shells and turning them into a special gift. The sounds of gently clinking shells is sure to attract fairies to a garden and remind you of the beach all year long.

YOU WILL NEED

Lightweight sea shells

3 18-inch pieces of thin, flat satin ribbon

A 10- to 12-inch-long smooth stick or dowel

1½ feet of dental floss

Scissors

White glue and a glue gun

INSTRUCTIONS

STEP 1: Tie on end of dental floss to each end of your stick. This is to hang your wind chimes.

STEP 2: Arrange your shells in several lines, three rows should be plenty. Now, using white glue or your glue gun, glue a line down the center of each shell and press the ribbon over the glue. Leave several inches free at the top of the ribbon to attach it to the dowel. Let the shell ribbons dry over night.

STEP 3: Tie the shell ribbons onto the stick and then hang it in a nice breezy spot on a deck or porch and enjoy the subtle music it creates.

CRAFTS FOR THE BIRD AND ANIMALS

ust as fairies love watching you showing kindness to your friends by giving gifts, they do the same thing with their dear friends the birds and the butterflies. Making projects that help to take care of those creatures is one more way to win the hearts of the fairy folk. But the absolute best part of making things for these winged creatures is that you will begin to see more of them so you will be able to continually marvel at their magical essence.

{ Bird Sipping Station }

(Adapted from Nature Smart)

This bird water fountain is an easy way to help the birds get a cool drink and take a break from flying. The only trick is to make sure that you keep the water nice and fresh so it doesn't become a home for mosquitos—a not so welcome bird substitute.

YOU WILL NEED

1 6-inch round plastic plant saucer

1 10-inch round plant saucer

Hole punch

16 thin straight branches (about a foot long)

6 feet of twine

Scissors

INSTRUCTIONS

STEP 1:   Punch 16 holes around the edge of the 10-inch saucer.

STEP 2:   Now weave the thin twigs through these holes. From the outside of the saucer, poke the end of a twig through any of the holes and then poke it through the fourth hole from the one you entered. Continue poking in the twigs and having them come through the fourth hole. You will need to have two twigs coming through one hole at the very end. If you need the holes to be bigger, use your hole punch to enlarge them a little by creating a neighboring hole.

STEP 3:   Cut three pieces of twine that measure about two feet. Punch three more holes around the rim of the saucer and tie these strings around these holes. Gather the three ends and tie them together so they are in one knot which you will use to hang from a tree.

STEP 4:   Place the smaller 6-inch saucer in the center of the twig covered saucer and fill it with water. The birds will perch on the interlacing twigs and sip away.

STEP 5:   Hang your water fountain from a high branch away from cats but in a place where you can access the water saucer easily.

{ Butterfly Feeder }

Giving a butterfly an extra dose of nectar serves two purposes; you are helping the butterflies refuel during their busy season and you get to be up close and personal to watch them dip their proboscises (butterfly tongues) into the nectar you have made for them. Once you get a hang of making these feeders, feel free to make more and share them with friends. The more we can help the butterflies, the better off the world will be.

YOU WILL NEED

Mason jar (and lid)

Kitchen sponge

Hammer and nail

Heavy-duty string

Sugar

Water

Scissors

Saucepan

Decorative washi tape and stickers

INSTRUCTIONS

STEP 1: Make your butterfly food by mixing together 9 parts water to 1 part sugar. In a small saucepan, bring the mixture to a boil until the sugar is completely dissolved. Let the sugar mixture cool completely.

STEP 2: Using a nail and hammer, have a grown up punch a small hole in the center of the mason jar lid.

STEP 3: Cut a ½-inch strip from your sponge, then pull it through the hole in the lid so about half of the sponge is sticking out from the top. This is tricky because the hole is small so you will need to tightly roll up the sponge and feed it through the hole.

STEP 4: Fill the jar with the sugar water, and make sure the sponge is soaked with the solution, but not dripping. (You can test to make sure your sponge fits correctly by putting water into the jar and turning it upside down. If it drips, you will need to cut a larger piece of sponge.)

STEP 4: Decorate your jar with washi tape and stickers.

STEP 5: Turn the jar upside down and tie some twine right below the lid. Cut two more pieces of string about two feet long. Take one end of one piece and tie it to the piece that is already secured around the neck of the jar. Then, attach the other end to the string on the opposite side of the jar. You will have created a nice loop so you can hang your feeder upside down. Tie the second length of string in the same way to make a second loop, perpendicular to the first. Place a final piece of twine through your two hanging loops to pull them together. Your jar should hang evenly.

STEP 7: To hang your feeder outside, place it about six inches higher than your tallest flowers or three feet down from a tree branch to make sure that the butterflies see it perfectly.

{ Cement Bird Bath }

irds and fairies, unlike some of you, actually like taking baths. There are many bird bath projects out there, several involving mosaic tiles. This one takes a bit of doing, but is quite amazing and sure to enchant a bird or a fairy into taking many baths. It is a true family project, however, so make sure you have your parents' blessing before you get your heart set on this, as they will need to be the ones mixing the concrete. Any time you see "quik-crete" in a project be forewarned that a handsome mess will ensue.

YOU WILL NEED

2 bags of Quick-Crete

Water

Mounds of slightly damp sand

1 or 2 tarps

Saran Wrap

Large rhubarb leaves

Tools to pour, stir, and contain the quick-crete

A log for the stand

INSTRUCTIONS

STEP 1: First lay a tarp down, then make a large mound of sand. Lay your rhubarb leaf over the sand mound, covering the entire pile as best you can.

STEP 2: Mix your quick-crete so that it is wet but firm. Pour Quick-Crete over the leaves in a thick layer, patting gently.

STEP 3: Cover your mound with a tarp and let dry for 1 to 2 weeks (depending on the weather). After it has had ample time to dry and harden, pull off the tarp and pull the molded concrete off the leaves. You will have a molded concrete leaf which can be place on a thick log. Fill your leaf-shaped bath with water and watch as the birds gather to clean themselves.

{ Fairy House Bird House }

his craft assumes the birds want to have their own fairy house too, and why wouldn't they? But that being said, the fairies and the birds can certainly share this and so it qualifies as a "two-fer." If you are particularly skilled as a woodworker, then perhaps you can make your own wooden bird house form. But if not, ready-made wooden birdhouses are available at most craft stores so that all you need to do is fair-ify it.

YOU WILL NEED

A bird house

Bark

Twigs

Moss

Shells

Dried flowers, leaves, and berries

Glue gun or tacky glue

INSTRUCTIONS

This is a pretty open-ended activity. Basically, you want to cover the boring old wooden bird house with all kinds of natural materials to make it look like a fairy house. Glue bark to the roof and side the walls with twigs and then glue on the other pieces from your collection so it will delight the birds and the fairies.

Making suet is more of a cooking activity than a craft, but once you've created your suet pudding, you can pour it in this tea cup converted suet holder and it then becomes crafty. The following recipe is pretty easy to make, but it does contain nuts so do not make this if you or anyone in your family has a peanut allergy.

{ Winter Pudding Recipe }

(Adapted from the North Carolina Bluebird Society)

YOU WILL NEED

2 quarts water

1 cup butter

4 cups grits (not instant)

1 cup peanut butter

Raisins

INSTRUCTIONS

In a large saucepan, bring water and butter to a boil. Slowly add grits, stirring and cooking until mixture begins to thicken. Remove from heat and add peanut butter and raisins. Stir well.

{ Tea Cup Holder }

YOU WILL NEED

Suet recipe above

An old tea cup

Short twig

Twine

INSTRUCTIONS

STEP 1: Pour the warm suet into an old coffee cup or tea cup. Keep an eye out at thrift stores or yard sales for old tea cups that you can use.

STEP 2: Once you have filled the cup with the suet and before it is completely hardened, push a twig into the suet across the cup from the handle. This will serve as the perch for the suet station.

STEP 3: Cut two long pieces of twine. Tie each piece to opposite sides of the tea cup handle and then tie them together to create a long loop. Hang the suet cup on a branch for the birds to sip on all winter.

{ Suet Cage Nesting Box }

Traditional suet holders can be purchased just about anywhere and chances are your family might already have one floating around. Often times, we run out of suet, as well as the time to make it again, and the lonely suet holder hangs with its wire cage empty. To quickly fill this void, you can fill the wire mesh with a variety of nesting materials to help the birds make their nests nice and cozy. Added bonus: you probably have lots of materials to use from all of your crafting endeavors.

YOU WILL NEED

Wire mesh suet feeder

Yarn scraps, wool roving, felt, dryer lint, and other soft fabric

INSTRUCTIONS

Simply cut the yarn and fabric scraps into small pieces and fill the wire cage. The birds will pull things out as needed. Keep an eye out for colorful nests around your neighborhood.

The Winter Tree

Feeding birds is an all-year endeavor, but the birds really need your help in the winter. To prepare for this, collect a bare branch with several offshoots. Plant this in a large pot of dirt. Some people even pour concrete to make it really sturdy, but I don't think this is necessary. Decorate your "tree" with all sorts of bird treat ornaments. Suet balls wrapped in ribbon, orange and grapefruit halves filled with suet, peanut-butter and bird-seed pine cones, rose hips threaded with twine, popcorn strings, and apple rings. Keep adding to your tree all winter and the birds will be well-fed and delighted. A great book that complements this project is *The Night Tree* by Eve Bunting, one of my absolute favorite winter books.

RESOURCES:

Green Guide for Artists: Nontoxic Recipes, Green Art Ideas & Resources for the Eco-Conscious Artist by Karen Michel

Fairy House: How to Make Amazing Fairy Furniture, Miniatures and More From Natural Materials by Mike and Debbie Schramer

Nature Crafts for Kids: 50 Fantastic Things to Make with Mother Nature's Help by Gwen Diehn and Terry Krautwurst

The Ultimate Book of Kid Concoctions by John E. Thomas and Danita Pagel

Making Peg Dolls by Margaret Bloom

Usborne Book of Fairy Things to Make and Do by Fiona Watt, Rebecca Gilpin and Leonie Pratt

Nature Smart: Awesome Projects to Make with Mother Nature's Help by Gwen Diehn, Terry Krautwurst, Alan Anderson, Joe Rhatigan, and Heather Smith

The Giant Book of Creativity for Kids by Bobbi Conner

Rainy Day Pastimes: 215 Ideas to Keep Children Happy edited by Magda Gray and Yvonne Deutch

Nature's Playground: Activities and Games to Encourage Children to Get Outdoors by Fiona Danks andJo Schofield

The Paper Playhouse: Awesome Art Projects for Kids Using Paper, Boxes, and Books by Katrina Rodabaugh

Dollhouse Magic: How to Make and Find Simple Dollhouse Furniture by P.K. Roche and John Knott

ACKNOWLEDGEMENTS

Glue is essential in most good craft projects, and it turns out to be essential in writing a craft book too. There were way more parts floating around with this book than any other and I owe the deepest thanks to Lynda Chilton for calmly securing those millions of pieces. Not only does she have a crafty eye, but she is endlessly patient, resourceful and exceedingly hardworking. Thank you, thank you! Without Michael Steere there would be no books, so thank you for your flexibility, sense of humor, and willingness to stay on the fairy train. Thank you to photographer Andy Dumas for your quick eye, patience, and for coming to the rescue time and time again.

I am also deeply grateful to all of the kids and families who help me fill these pages with adorable fairy models! It is a unique joy to watch you all grow up through these pages and it wouldn't be nearly as fun without your smiles and willingness to dig right in to the projects.

So thank you to cover girl, Ami, Graham, Marguerite, Izzy, Zoe, and their families for bringing so much magic to the Children's Chapel shoot. Ella, Klara, Lila, Amelia, Ava, and Midge for making Merryspring's Fairy festival even brighter. Tessa, Andy, Midge, Clark, and Gwen were great sports through a very long photo shoot and smiled through it all. Thank you to Mrs. Peter's Gifted and Talented Origami Experts for walking me through the challenging but amazing world of origami. Thank you to the Compass Rose Fairy Camp kids for trying all this stuff out and for such exuberant belief in the fairy world. Ava and Daphne, thank you for always being up for a last minute photo session again and again since the very beginning.

I want to especially thank my mom, for instilling in me her love of tiny things and for all of those days spent making salt-dough, dioramas and pouring through the *Rainy Day Craft Book* for new ideas to try. Thank you to Phoebe and Daphne for a constant stream of creativity and beautiful mess-making. You are both true artists and I love watching your creative spirits unfold. And to Jeff, you are the glue that holds us in one piece.